Sight and Insight

By the same author

300 Years of American Painting
Proud Youth

ALEXANDER ELIOT

Sight and Insight

McDOWELL, OBOLENSKY INC.
Publishers *New York*

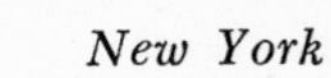

Library of Congress Catalog No.: 59-7119

 Published in New York by McDowell, Obolensky Inc. and simultaneously in the Dominion of Canada by George J. McLeod, Limited, Toronto.

Manufactured in the United States of America by Quinn & Boden Company, Inc., Rahway, New Jersey.

Designed by Leonard W. Blizard

The Library of Congress has catalogued this book as follows:

Eliot, Alexander.
Sight and insight. New York, McDowell, Obolensky [1959]

191 p. 22 cm.

1. Art—Philosophy. 2. Art—Addresses, essays, lectures. I. Title.

N79.E4 701 59–7119 ‡

Library of Congress

With you, Jane

Contents

Sight and Insight

Chapter 1

A Room with a View in the City of Art

FROM A DISTANCE THE CITY OF ART SEEMS RINGED with battlements, but those are gates, not walls.

Everybody goes there for a visit sometime. The whirlwind tour is popular. Some visitors prefer making a deep study of two or three streets. But the way to enjoy the city of art thoroughly is to take a room there and stay a while. One stands at the high window, a single free spirit brooding over all the ages and the grandest things mankind has made.

The city lies wide open to all. There on the terrace paces the archeologist with his tape measure. Down that alley ducks a growing boy, deadpan, on the lookout for nudes. A crowd is entering the cathedral. In the bank of ages a numismatist polishes coins. Children climb a statue in the park, and on the bench nearby a beaded African whittles an idol. Two lovers steal a kiss, meanwhile, in an Egyptian tomb. All sorts of people are treating the city as if they owned it, and they do.

The city of art is mankind's common creation, common property and common ground.

Bohemia is the city's factory district. At first it seems only glitter and darkness, a shadowy seething up the narrow twisted streets. On a balcony a girl is trying to dry her long shining hair by moonlight. One climbs to a loft, lit by a neon sign outside, where a painter with a name that no one seemed to catch howls hello and turning stabs at his canvas with glistening brush. Time to eat the still-life.

Much has been said about Bohemia—romantic on the one side, scornful on the other. Yet one of the best things about it is seldom mentioned: the healthy appetite one finds there. Bohemianism is the defiant indulgence of appetite for life. Let mystics murmur against having to eat: let philosophers frown at having to sleep: the artist remains ravenous for life in every shape, from meat to dreams. The artist comes hungry, happy and wondering into the world. He is like the traveler who knocked one night on the door of a shadowy mansion, and found himself admitted to a great hall, warm with log fires and alive with candlelight, the guests assembled and a great feast spread.

It is better to receive than to give—up to a point. After that point the reverse is equally true. In fact there comes a time when if a man is not a source he is a sewer. The true artist has disciplined and filled and freed himself for giving. He is a bottomless cup that keeps welling full and running over.

Picasso told of walking in the Tuileries, getting "filled up with green," and then going home to paint a green abstraction.

Max Gubler put the artist's attitude to life in a word. It is a "bear-hug."

Built by such generous enthusiasts, the city of art is naturally filled with delights. But it can be overwhelming at first. Best start with the minor wonders. Masterpieces will wait. Such-and-such may be an inspiration when the right time comes. Meanwhile the man who follows his own taste remains his own master. His tread is sure. Still, a masterpiece is a masterpiece. Sooner or later one's gaze and the gaze of one's mind will be drawn to it. This changes everything. It is as if one had passed through a series of infatuations to find true love. One comes to feel the same true love for every masterpiece, and what a multitude awaits! Time was when a man had to wangle invitations to see them in private palaces, and tip the butler besides. Today nine-tenths of great art is in public collections, on public view. It lies open to millions: immeasurable wealth, a feast for the soul such as no pope nor emperor could ever dream of seeing for himself, until the present age.

Therefore, one imagines, art must be more widely enjoyed than ever before. But no. An hour spent observing the visitors in any great museum proves the opposite: art is more widely abhorred than ever before. The wonder is, why do so many people go out of their way to abhor it? They flock through the galleries like lost souls looking for an escape hatch. Or like hungry travelers in a forest of forbidden fruit. They communicate in reverent mutterings and hopeless, half-completed gestures, meant to say that certain works are "beautiful" or "interesting." Meanwhile their restless eyes are saying it is all poison.

As they deny the pictures, so the pictures deny them: the branches spring up and the fruit flies out of reach. This invisible process can be seen reflected in museum faces again and again. It is a funny thing to watch, and sad as well. Disappointed again and again, the dutiful visitor progresses from feelings of obscure hurt, to frustration, to blushing anger and unspoken abhorrence of all art. Then he leaves the gallery, having done his duty. But the dutiful are pilloried enough. They have been given bad consciences, and that is their main trouble.

Amongst the miserable throng in any great gallery, perhaps one man in twenty looks surprisingly well pleased. From picture to picture he steps, as lightly and sedately as a flamingo. Often he leans down to peer, smiling, at the labels. He carries his arms akimbo and tilts his head back as if he were tasting something sweet. There treads a pharisee. If he gets any real pleasure it is not from art but from what he knows about the subject. He is like a botanist describing the forbidden fruits of the forest. Now and then he may take a taste of one, a mere nibble, just to be sure he has its name right. But he would never dream of actually eating one down. For him, as for the philistine, art remains forbidden.

There is no harm in the pharisees either, unless one elects to follow them. But the only way to begin to understand art is to accept it whole-heartedly on one's own, and then to enjoy it. The Spanish peasant drinking from a wineskin or a *cantaro* never sips; he lets the wine spurt right down his gullet. Only afterwards will he reflect on its satisfying taste, the warm feeling in his belly and the new beauty of things round about. That is the way to enjoy art. Let questions of taste and scholarship—philistine preferences and pharisaical opinions—come later.

Just as between two people, so between a man and a masterpiece: direct emotional experience is best. When a man approaches great art in the same open, sympathetic spirit he brings to close friends, he will enjoy it. No one ever truly saw a masterpiece without enjoyment. The city of art itself would be no more than a mirage, a dream, if not enjoyed. One who failed to enjoy it has never been near it. But the man who had a great time in the city, and came to love it, carries it with him everywhere forever. It has built into his mind. Its secret places and its monuments alike will shine for him at midnight, or move like shade across the blaze of noon. The eye of his imagination opens, and he rejoices.

Yet how few have this experience! Art means less to intelligent people at present than sex does to worker ants. The city of art, the most glorious city ever built, with room for all mankind, is in danger of becoming a ghost-town.

Perhaps the path of free enjoyment and personal interpretation can help lead men back to the city. At least it demonstrates that art belongs to them. To all who have eyes, art offers a flashing multitude of insights. Some of these insights the interpreter shapes into words and offers over again. He does not work dogmatically but as a friend in conversation, exactly as if he were describing people or landscapes that had inspired him.

Elder critics are agreed that "plastic values"—pleasing combinations of abstract forms—matter most in art. They demonstrate their kind of sensibility by analyzing compositions, and dismissing "the vulgar emotions of life." This is not what is needed now. To interpret art in a more personal and emotional way is not to deny its abstract qualities—or any other qualities. It means responding as a whole human being to a whole work of art. Afterwards one tries to answer the question: "What does this particular creation mean to me?" The reply is never final, but felt. One is simply passing around his private telescope, among friends, at a window overlooking the city.

One thing the interpreter knows for sure is that every masterpiece has spiritual significance. One and all, they come from above the snow-line of experience. Yet they speak to man directly, since every single human being is engaged in spiritual struggle. A man may never have set foot inside a church door, nor read a word of philosophy, yet will he contemplate last things. Everybody thinks about the aims and the end of this life, many times.

Art meanwhile is thought to be a world apart, with its own government and rules and mysteries of its own. It is a darkness hard to penetrate, one might suppose. But the true mystery is that there are no mysteries in art. Or rather, there are just the central and eternal mysteries of life itself. Every masterpiece concerns these mysteries, and so will any true philosophy of art.

If most people are blind to art now, it is because they have been taught to see it out of context. The right context of art is the context of human life. It is the struggle to create a happier and wiser man.

Seen in this context, art is no darkness but a light.

Chapter 2

The Children of Light

THE LOVELIEST THING ABOUT THE CITY OF ART IS the play of light across and within it—sunbeams, cloud-shadows, quicksilver dusk, fireworks, searchlights and starry heaven at the high window.

All artists, including sculptors, are children of light. They labor in, with and through light, always light; they shape their work to give light back again. Velásquez' light is like transparent golden bees swarming the honeyed shadow, while Rogier van der Weyden's is like water over marble. Picasso's light seizes, smears and shapes a dark core.

An artist's feeling about light is central to his creations. So central that a broad stylistic shift in the handling of light will reflect a shift in the whole culture. The great masters not only express but also inspire such changes. For example, Leonardo, Caravaggio, and Rembrandt show a succession of ground-swells in European thought.

Leonardo kept roving and puzzling, yet in general he saw the powers of light and darkness as twins, equally matched and locked in an eternal struggle. Thus he looked back to the dualism of pagan thought and forward to the dualism of scientific thought. In his own day such dualism smacked of witchcraft; it was considered evil. Yet by inventing chiaroscuro to express it, Leonardo bent the path of art, and thought as well, his way.

Chiaroscuro figures are shaped of light and shadow only. Contours blur like smoke upon the air. Caverns open, spun with luminous webs. The twins of light and darkness fight a running battle over the forms—the lights splashed and soothed with shadows, and the shadows crowned, spiked, shimmering with lights.

The most concentrated example of this is the *Mona Lisa*. Her face is formed entirely of light and shade: what seems to be flesh is only a mingling of vast inhuman forces. Did Leonardo love her? Did he not! He took her picture with him into death. Only she was not a lady who posed so much as a spirit that waited. Within the *Mona Lisa* sits Leonardo's goddess. It is Sophia, spirit of Eternal Wisdom, who deigns to shine darkly through this smiling, troubled pool of light and shade. It is all understanding in a single half-unwilling and half-human glance.

Light and shadow were also equally pleasing to Caravaggio, yet he did not treat them as living forces. What he liked was just their usefulness in illuminating his own passions: flesh and faith. So he turned Leonardo's chiaroscuro into a kind of stage-lighting, relatively hard and still. He was factual—not in the scientific, analyzing sense but in the Spanish manner, sensuous and austere. *Es esto,* his art keeps saying: "that's how it is."

As the model for his *Dormition of the Virgin* at the Louvre, Caravaggio chose the swollen corpse of a whore dredged from the Tiber. The canvas fairly swells with dumb and gloomy devotion: faith to him was just as factual as flesh. The Spanish spirit of the Counter-Reformation had conquered him along with the rest of Italy.

As their titles suggest, Caravaggio's best pictures represent transition, opportunity, and not consummation. *The Conversion of Saint Paul* shows a man stricken with light, felled flat. His horse waits patiently. *The Calling of Saint Matthew* shows Jesus pointing along a ray of light to the one man among a band of ruffians who refuses to look up. A handsome and hopeful boy nearby, who makes a "who, me?" gesture, has been generally mistaken for Matthew. But the saint, scrabbling his coins in sullen fury at the head of the table, is where the light goes.

A black clamor threads the stillness of these canvases, as comets thread the cold of outer space.

By contrast to Caravaggio, Rembrandt reflects the Bible-reading Protestant position. Both the Old and New Testaments come roaring and humming through his art as the sea roars and hums in a sea shell. Still more important is the fact that Rembrandt darkens nature herself in order to assign greater lights to man. His figures live in shadow; they shine from within. Their inborn light is saying that God needs no intermediaries but works directly in the souls of men. For example, Rembrandt's *Peter Betraying Christ,* at Amsterdam, is no strong man turned coward, no darkened rock, but rather a very opal of light. Christ in the distance, turning to look back, fills him with divinity even now.

Fra Angelico, who was perhaps the purest of Catholic painters, kept saying: "Not me, not you, for neither of us matters; but only Christ and the love of Christ." Rembrandt, Protestant, says: "Not me but Christ in me, and not you but Christ in you."

Riding an elevator can give rise to an uneasy feeling that time has stopped . . . caused partly by the blind vertical motion and partly by the absence of daylight. Natural lights are twined with time. Daylight moves and changes with the sun and sky. Candlelight and firelight dance gladly on their own graves. But electric light remains the same. Natural lights caress, in short, while artificial light impinges.

Van Gogh had mastery of a dozen kinds of light. Who has painted starlight more convincingly? With his *Night Café* at Arles he made a mothlike rush at artificial light. In a letter to his brother, Van Gogh described what he came up against: "The terrible passions of humanity." The billiard table changed into a green crouching beast, in a red lair. But color, not light, is the protagonist here.

Who has yet painted a great picture of an electrically lit interior, with light itself as the hero? Hopper's *Night Hawks,* at the Chicago Art Institute, might be a candidate. But its great strength lies in the dramatic equation made between the lunchroom pie-wedge of brightness and the dark street outside. Artificial light and natural dark are given equal weight. The dark is the less lonely.

Wire a cathedral for electricity, and at once its high dark places wince into gloom. Obscure chapels that used to welcome the penitent will look at him no more. He kneels alone, rumpled and sick, beneath a naked electric bulb. Electricity, as much as bombs, has turned the great cathedrals into monuments.

Each created atom, said the ancients, reflects God's light in its degree: all things are lights. But this is not the sort of thought that occurs to a man in an elevator, a bar, a lunchroom or a wired chapel.

Vermeer believed it.

This mild genius suspended the war between light and

darkness, gave the victory to light, and made light a manifestation of loving-kindness. Even when stealing into Vermeer's darkest interior by a narrow window, light is welcomed as a lover. The far corners whisper hello to light. Instead of humping their backs like angry cats the shadows under the furniture are purring. A lady smooths a tablecloth: light smooths it for her and gently holds her hand upon it, saying, "This usual busy morning is forever."

Light barely touches, without moving, the pearl in the lady's ear. Now the light rounds her cheek. As merrily as breathing, it kisses her parted lips. Light invades her eyes. She glances back through the ages from light's bodiless embrace.

For Vermeer, light was not just a vehicle of love, it was love. Vermeer loved light itself even more than what it touched, yet it carries a personal caress to everything he pictures. He preferred painting women, therefore, and interiors steeped in peaceful doings. Men he avoided picturing, or else averted their faces. Nature, that stormy deep, he kept beyond the dikes.

For his choice of subject matter, Vermeer has been called a genre painter, and even been thoroughly confused on occasion with the genre master de Hooch. There is a lovely mysteriousness about de Hooch, true, yet nothing like Vermeer's. De Hooch points in fancy to the far side of the seen, of the familiar, which one feels is bound to be unveiled in good time. One fancies that the wineglass in a canvas by de Hooch will soon be filled and emptied once again. The girl will get a little tipsy and may even find herself seduced, but it is more likely that an aunt will arrive and rescue her.

How different is Vermeer! Will the milk ever fill that dish? Will that smiling girl ever frown or sigh, or turn away at last? No, not ever. The mystery in Vermeer waits not to be unraveled or imagined but to reveal itself—in the eternity of the moment when light first touched it.

Titian's forms and colors are not touched by light but drenched with it. In his *Bacchanal* at the Prado, for example, the result is a reversal of Vermeer's. Instead of bringing heaven down to earth, Titian lifts the earth into heaven. Instead of showing the eternal in a moment, he shows a moment in the eternal. Vermeer creates a sense of tremulous permanence; Titian creates one of eternal passage.

Vermeer was a citizen of Delft—that calm, pearly town, won from the deep. Titian was a citizen of Venice—where light fleets, colors shine through each other, the very palaces waver, and one prays for the high, sunset glow to hold, if only for a moment more.

Looking at the *Bacchanal,* with its tawny glow of afternoon in September, and a high cloud and the sail of a parting ship giving back the last of the sun's glory, one asks, "Do I wake or sleep?" and then forgets the question in the looking; one turns swiftly back from thought to vision, from abstraction to the real *Bacchanal,* fearing that its light may have dimmed already in the moment lost.

As with all true miracles, the evanescent glow of Titian's *Bacchanal* is not only amazing but also significant. It gives, as was intended, new depth and resonance to the pagan injunction: "Eat, drink and be merry, for tomorrow you may die." This is not in itself a profound thing to say. One man may say it with a belch, another with a bellow; one with a self-pitying sigh and another with a song of praise. Titian said it with a lifetime's work. It will be said again, always. D. H. Lawrence was echoing its classic overtones precisely when he wrote: "Whatever the dead may know, they cannot know the joys of being alive in the flesh."

Monet, poring over the light on Rouen Cathedral, saw not an edifice of eternal hope but rather a vision of the ephemeral. "This stone façade," his paintings seem to say, "is rosy as flesh, delicate as hair, and fading fast with the fading light, crumbling into shadow." At his easel Monet was a frenzied athlete holding back the dusk. He begged mankind to witness a beauty on the edge of being lost. Not that he lacked faith in the morning: he knew the sun would rise again—and set again—but not for every man, not forever for any man, not very long for anyone.

Just as Casanova predicted with each love affair his own inevitable impotence and death, so Monet kept predicting with each passionate canvas his own blindness and death. Monet wept; he saw nature magnified and made iridescent by his tears. Profoundly sensuous people are apt to be either mad or sad.

Even Titian was sad. Right beside his *Bacchanal* hangs the profile of a vigorous, refined old man—himself. He looks away calmly. This silver-bearded aristocrat was once a boy along with Giorgione in Giovanni Bellini's studio. Then for many, many decades after Bellini's death and Giorgione's early death, Titian had ruled supreme in Venice. His closest friends were among the wisest and liveliest men of that harvest-time, and great kings, too, made pilgrimages to see Titian. His fame filled the Christian world. That so gifted, loved and fortunate a man should think on death, is natural.

If all men fall alike before the face of death, they are also alike in possessing certain inalienable rights—and yet they are not at all equal in worthiness. To pretend that artists of Titian's size are doomed to the same disappointments and eventual uselessness as other men is to deny the saving grace of art itself. The great creators are not momentary, white-capped waves, however towering upon the seas of history, but sailors, admirals indeed, masters of their voyages. They sail upon history, including the history of thought and style, as upon the ocean sea. They are the admirals discovering ever-new Americas at the world's edge —that is, before the face of death.

There is no cheating death, yet one may build a fire of love and glory before the darkness. One may celebrate beautifully, peacefully, lovingly, completely, the joys of life. Ovid said this in a single line: "Ripeness is all."

Unlucky men look forward to death as a release. For the faithful it spells judgment, and heaven for the hopeful. And then for serious sensualists of Titian's sort, death means first of all the loss of life. Casanova, Titian's countryman, went remembering into the dragon's lair, and chuckling a little. D. H. Lawrence went darkly, yet boldly. "Prepare," he wrote towards the end, "oh, prepare thy ship of death!" Dylan Thomas swarmed in roaring. Instead of calling upon the personal champion against death, who is Christ, all of these men invoked one or both of the classical champions: poetry and reason. "Eat, drink and be merry, for tomorrow you may die. Whatever the dead may know, they cannot know the joys of being alive in the flesh. Ripeness is all." These thoughts come together, they become one, in Titian's *Bacchanal*.

In the picture's tremulous glow people are dancing together, singing together, talking together. They are weaving a oneness of these activities, weaving it around the wine, which some scoop from the sacred spring and others carry and pour. The man toward the center who lifts the wine like an offering and gazes at the sunlight streaming through it may personify Titian himself, for he has the artist's approach. The hunter alone with his dog in the distance also is served; in this idyll one may sit apart and still participate. Not even sleep separates these people; the dozing girl in the foreground might be dreaming the entire festival, so much a part of it is she.

The boldest stroke may be the little boy who daintily lifts his tunic to pee in the sacred wine. What might have been a comic or a jarring note is part of the sweetly serious unity. A picture's details can be all-important. One should not hesitate to lose oneself in them. One can easily step back afterwards and see the picture whole again. Stepping back from this particular detail, for example, one finds childhood caught up into the adult world, as it should be. Furthermore, the wine is proved so holy that nothing can corrupt it.

The old man on the far hilltop lifts his head and points as if to say, "All this between me on my hill and you who are outside the vision is meaningful." He is like the voice one sometimes hears in dreams—solemn, imperative, calling one by name—which gives the dream's whole meaning. The wine seems to be flowing from the old man's hill. Is it really his blood, and is he a sacrifice to the general joy? Does this hoary-bearded man represent the waning year, and his blood the harvest thereof? Or is he the priest-king of the *Golden Bough,* the human sacrifice that was offered in fertility rites around the savage world? Or is he a pagan god, simply, and is this the twilight of the gods —a last fling? Finally, and most strangely, does he speak for the God of the Christians? "Take ye and drink; this is my blood." And, "A new commandment give I unto you, that ye love one another."

All of these combined interpretations would have been natural to Titian's time and temperament. Modern science tends to treat as superstition the myths and rituals that

Renaissance humanism regarded as vessels of eternal, though disguised, wisdom.

Is not one interpretation of the *Bacchanal* preferable to all the rest? No, a masterpiece is multiform, and speaks differently to different hearts. At last, in the presence of the picture itself, the many-tongued murmur of interpretation ceases altogether. Titian has painted a miraculous harmony of mortals. He has proved that this harmony, this health of soul, this happiest aspiration of mankind, is possible. It has to be, since he himself could visualize it and since other men, gazing at his *Bacchanal,* can understand.

He has pictured men and women weaving their light together with the fading light, calmly and happily holding their mutual love aloft before the face of death, pouring and drinking life's holy wine, blessed for now, each one, and forever as mankind.

Chapter 3

The Latent Content of a Masterpiece

MASTERPIECES USUALLY TELL STORIES. THAT IS, they illustrate ideas that can be understood apart from the artist's deepest intention. On the other hand, masterpieces always possess an abstract splendor that can be appreciated quite apart from their actual subject. Some people therefore see art as illustration and others see it as abstraction. Both are seeing surfaces only. It is true that one has to begin with surfaces—the surface beauties of a masterpiece and also its surface meanings. But these surface qualities of story and composition are only the manifest content of a masterpiece.

Far within lies the latent content—at the point where illustration and abstraction merge.

Any masterpiece will prove the point. Leonardo's *Saint Jerome* at the Vatican looks every inch a saint, and his attendant lion is a lion absolutely. That is good illustration. Also the forms of the saint and the lion are brilliantly counterpointed and their contours filled with interlocking life. That is good abstraction. Both together make the picture a masterpiece, for when its illustrative and abstract qualities are permitted to merge in one's mind, something marvelous appears, something new in art.

Before Leonardo, pictures of Saint Jerome had made the lion at worst a mere symbol and at best a mere pet. Leonardo not only allows him to become real but also gives him equal weight with the saint, binding them together in a composition that is perfect and complete. From this the latent content comes. It is that the saint and the lion are one. The saint partakes of the lion's power and passion while the lion partakes of the saint's calm faith.

Leonardo himself was both leonine and saintly. He could actually twist horseshoes in his hands, and he used to buy caged birds in order to set them free. Almost everybody has something of the lion and something of the saint inside himself, but usually the two are at odds. Therefore by showing the saint and the lion to be real companions in his picture, Leonardo points a way for men to heal themselves. He is not didactic, however. He moves the heart more than the mind. Instead of illustrating a precept, his *Saint Jerome* lives as a subtly inspiring example to sick mankind—just as he intended.

Why did Leonardo not make his meaning plainer, or at least explain it in his title? A masterpiece should give its message clearly, no? Why do they make these things so hard to understand? One hears these questions constantly, and yet the answer is not far to seek.

A poster gives its message right off. It was designed to be seen at a glance. But a masterpiece is meant to be experienced, to go to the heart of a man. A masterpiece has to be taken whole into the depths of consciousness and, so to speak, re-created there. It shines in the dark chamber of the heart. Mere knowledge may be picked up anywhere, but understanding comes only from experience. A masterpiece, however, is meant as an experience. Until it is experienced it is not understood.

Really to experience a Leonardo can be painful, for it stretches consciousness. Therefore one is tempted to stop with the manifest content of his picture and dote on that. One speaks of his "technique" and of his "mystery"—seldom of his truth. Leonardo has never been taken seriously enough. He shows the infinite in the flesh.

The *Virgin and Saint Anne* at the Louvre represents a woman sitting in another woman's lap to watch a baby bestride a lamb. Or does it? The difficulties that the picture has raised for Freud, amongst others, results from efforts to analyze this manifest content.

The impassive splendor of Saint Anne should be enough to show that here is no mere woman. She is more than a saint, besides. She looks as if she could embrace the whole world without even caring about it. This "Saint Anne" is really infinite Wisdom. The Virgin hovering in Wisdom's lap and reaching down to Christ is pure feeling, all love. More than the historical Virgin she is eternal tenderness, reaching out and giving everything. The infant Christ, so new, is not only Christ in the flesh but in the spirit also. He is eternal Becoming. He shows his mother what He will do, which is to keep on becoming the Lamb of God.

The softly downward and inward spiraling of these figures—from the infinite and eternal to the sacrificial present—takes place at the calm center of a cosmic whirlwind.

But how about a masterpiece without any such mystical overtones? Will it also have a latent content?

At the Prado, *The Drinkers* by Velásquez compares in power to Titian's nearby *Bacchanal*. But to step from the

Titian to the Velásquez is like awakening from a lovely dream to find oneself stretched out on a bench in a tavern garden. In the Titian, space and atmosphere were more ideal than real, with just the right amount of room for each figure to move freely and all of them enveloped in the balmy, glowing, swiftly darkening air as in a festival of love. By contrast, in the Velásquez space and atmosphere are impersonal, indifferent: a rectangle filled precisely to the brim with clear, strong afternoon light. The figures merely occupy the place; without them it would look the same. And instead of seeming ideal they are brutally real.

No one imagined these people: they were hired to pose. They are worn, sunburnt peasants, neither handsome nor ugly, posing, play-acting, with Spanish gusto and a hint of mockery. "This is a silly business," their faces say, "but perhaps there is a drink in it for us." One of them kneels before a half-naked Bacchus who gazes smilingly to one side, out of the picture, as if inviting the approval of an unseen presence.

It comes as a shock to realize that the peasants who stare straight out of the picture are gazing not towards the artist but into a mirror. Their expressions say as much. Whenever one person consciously looks at another, a certain liveliness comes into his eyes, a reflection of the other person's life. So with the boy-Bacchus. The doubting, half-smiling dullness of the central figure—the man who holds the bowl in which wine tilts and glances—is very different. This doubting dullness overtakes all men who look into mirrors, as if they wondered whether the reflection could really be themselves. Children, naturally, know that it is not. Observe a little boy in a barber's chair, howling and wriggling, red-faced. Well he knows that it is not in the mirror his shorn hair falls, but down his neck.

Velásquez disposed his group, a large mirror and his

easel in a triangle, so that he could glance between them all at will. A less determined realist than Velásquez might have chiefly studied the people before him, trying by subjective means to get beneath the appearances shown in the mirror. Or, he might have paid most attention to his canvas, multiplying details and mixing radiant hues, trying by art to clarify or improve what the mirror showed. Not Velásquez; he painted bluntly, broadly, impassively, and as darkly as the mercurial mirrors of his time, picturing just what his mirror saw. He does not pry, he does not gloss, he reflects. Yet his reflections overflow with meaning.

Velásquez hired a youth to play-act the part of Bacchus, and he purposely makes plain the fact that it is just an act. In Titian's *Bacchanal* the wine came from another world beside which this is a prison, and it unlocked the prison doors. Velásquez' wine is simply wine: a cheering but unstable factor in human life. It is human life that counts for Velásquez. Man is the vessel that contains and gives meaning to bread and wine and godliness and all the rest. Man, says Velásquez, is like a god. He tills and sows and reaps; he grins and breaks the furniture; he loves and he may sleep a while but he never dies.

Such is the latent content of Velásquez' masterpiece. Humanism, dark, blunt and polished like a riflebutt—humanism always was the burden of Velásquez' philosophy. People are the truth, he says: these people.

Latent content can be damned ugly sometimes, though never in a masterpiece. Perhaps this should go without saying. Everyone has seen examples of it in life, such as when a glutton says grace at table.

In painting, two brief examples will suffice: both turn-of-the-century favorites at the Tate Gallery in London.

They are Sir Luke Fildes' *The Doctor* and Watts' equally famous *Hope*. The doctor sitting in the gloom by the bedside of a sick child is insufferably noble and so is the picture as a whole. Beneath the dark and treacly nobility of its manifest content there beats a heart of stone, so smug. This doctor ought to be a fat black spider spinning a shroud for the child. *Hope* sits enthroned upon the slippery globe of this Earth, blindfolded, holding a broken harp in the twilight, wetly mantled, drooping, altogether in a blue funk. One could kick her.

Is there any harm in latent content such as this? It is even a little amusing. And yet harmful. Because to experience, without rejecting, the latent content of *The Doctor* is to share as a smug partner, consciously or not, in something fatuous. Likewise to experience as in a dream, without a smile, the hopelessness of Watts' *Hope,* will sap one's own. Because if that is the girl, there can be no earthly use in calling upon her for help at any time.

The latent content of a masterpiece, however, does nothing but good. A masterpiece is always a good experience. And one need not recognize its latent content to get the good of it. The good comes in the experiencing. Then afterwards if one can think it through, so much the better.

Nobody can prove that the latent content of a masterpiece is always beneficial and never ugly, yet every time one comes upon an exception to this rule further study shows either that the work in question is absurdly overrated—quite often a forgery—or else that one had not yet reached the heart of it.

To take what might seem a difficult case, is not the latent content of Goya's nightmare and war pictures ugly? Is he not using ugliness to point to ugliness, and bitterness to arouse bitterness? No, even to find him bitter is to stop at the manifest content of Goya's heroic art.

There is a Goya at the Prado of two men up to their knees in quicksand, in the wilderness, clubbing each other to death. Each man seems to believe that by killing the other he may somehow save himself. Yet death is for all and there is quicksand in the bed of the river of life.

The surface beauties of this fresco are almost overwhelming. An austere, silver-dark splendor surrounds and imbues the bloody combatants. But unless one's appreciation of the surface is balanced by recognition of the subject, one may fall into a sissified drifting and dreaming before the picture. It is real, after all, as well as beautiful.

Fighting hurts. These men are in a rage of agony. They cry out to God against each other, across the crunch and thudding of blows. Murderers, they are hell-bound together.

Such is the picture's manifest content, which one needs no aesthetic sense to grasp. In fact, manifest content can usually be recognized in a post-card reproduction. Not so latent content, which partakes of both illustrative and pictorial values. Latent content lies in what the artist actually did, not only what he thought or what he proposed to do. It steeps the physical presence of the picture itself. But the only way to find it lies in perusing the picture's illustrative and aesthetic meanings together, until they merge. At the moment of their merging, the latent content may appear.

To say in picture form that fighting hurts is easy. Al Capp's cartoons do that every other week. To say that mortal combat between grown men is madness, takes a little more art. Still, scores of painters have accomplished it. To say all this and say as well that men are brothers—needs Goya.

"All men are brothers." Such is the latent content of Goya's picture. It seems to contradict the manifest content while actually illuminating it—as often happens in dreams and masterpieces.

But how did Goya accomplish this? Precisely by the tension he creates between the picture's awesome beauty and the ugliness it illustrates. These murderous men are pictured as parts of a harmony infinitely greater and more compelling than their own disharmony. One feels that if only they had the least idea where they were and who they were—or if one could somehow get through and tell them—they would instantly fall upon each other's necks to beg forgiveness as true brothers, children of God.

Chapter 4

The Artist's Purpose

WHAT MAKES AN ARTIST? WHAT LEADS HIM TO create? Sympathetic understanding of art—the only kind there is—requires an answer to this thorny question.

The men who view art from above assume its motivations are self-centered if not ulterior. Economists, for example, tend to regard art as a commodity, luxury-class, produced for *money* in response to demand. History proves that just as money follows power art follows money. Moreover, the main purposes of private collections are first to parade and second to insure their owners' wealth. Collectors are apt to be rich. But does this make artists mercenary?

It is true, for example, that seventeenth century Dutch painting answered the tastes and pretensions of a dominant burgher class. Yet how explain its crowning light: Vermeer? Genius is always unexpected. No one commissioned Vermeer to perform his miracles. Nobody could, for until he himself imagined them they were unimaginable.

His contemporaries apparently preferred the more anecdotal Pieter de Hooch. Vermeer's few surviving works, however, are now among the most valuable pictures in existence. Prices reflect not only the market and the fashion but also the spiritual needs of different ages. De Hooch gave dignity to the most casual happenings of his own time. Vermeer shone his mother-of-pearl Lowland light into eternity. His ray enters the twentieth century like a blessing, made all the more precious by present darkness and violence.

Questions of price keep intruding on art: they can hardly be avoided. Anyway, money matters can help clarify larger ones. A canvas that Rembrandt could not sell at all now brings over a million dollars. On the other hand a vast cavalry charge that went far to make Meissonier rich and famous can now be had for a song. The truth is that neither the Rembrandt nor the Meissonier ever possessed the slightest financial value in itself—only in the market. The values of art in itself are either spiritual or nonexistent.

Titian lived like a lord, old Rembrandt like a hideaway, Gauguin like a bum. No one knows what Vermeer got for his pictures. Everybody knows what Van Gogh got: nothing. So much for the money motive. Artists come into the world not to fill their own bellies but to bring new nourishment to mankind.

Yet they have to find a little money somehow in order to live and work. This is what is laughingly called a "social problem." It has nothing to do with art, luckily, for it has baffled the ages. A recurrent solution to this, as to most social problems, is slavery. One of the great masters of Indian miniature painting used to sign himself, *The Slave of Thy Threshold,* adding thoughtfully—*called "The Immortal."*

Power is something that artists have in abundance; only theirs operates inwardly; it is hidden, and seldom hurtful. To shape diverse and recalcitrant materials into something whole, harmonious and radiant is a supremely powerful act. It takes a fighting spirit, a sense of pleasure in struggle against odds. Benvenuto Cellini—who loved precious, sparkling things, was great at casting in metals and created fiery figures—remains by his own account the very archetype of aggressive artist. Michelangelo got his nose smashed in a brawl. Smashing at marble he did better.

Neither Napoleon invading Russia nor Tolstoy writing *War and Peace* had the power to do precisely what he liked with his project: however, Tolstoy was the better off, and he knew it.

"If you're looking for something to be brave about," said Robert Frost, "consider the fine arts." This motive has been underestimated. Neither sport nor war but art is the deepest channel for aggressive instincts, for the will to power. And art's laurels last.

So power leads to *glory*—which exerts a powerful attraction of its own. Artists yearn for fame, as tax collectors, for example, do not. Here, as in aggressiveness, artists resemble athletes and military men. The hungry prize-fighter or the second lieutenant on the eve of battle and the sculptor arranging his first exhibition are alike borne up by dreams of glory. They aim to distinguish themselves.

Yet once it has been satisfied the yearning for glory begins losing force. Champions and generals prefer victory to glory, and masters prefer masterpieces. Michelangelo refused all honorific titles except "Sculptor." Plain old "Michelangelo" suited him fine.

Love—nude models and all that—also inspires the beginning artist. Appreciation helps keep him going, when and if he gets it. Correggio once was offered a good sum to embellish the dome of a cathedral. When he had done the job the authorities expressed grim disappointment. They paid him off all right, every cent, but all in coppers. Striving to lug the great sack home, Correggio died of heart-failure—or perhaps of a broken heart. He may have hoped to get a little love with his fee.

No, but love is the wrong thing to expect from any kind of work. Love comes after hours.

Frustrations are the turbines of art: so says the psychologist. Being unfit for sociable communication, it is argued, the artist tries to express his guilty passions in pictures or sculptures. Freudians—who are crazy—insist that the frustration be purely sexual. In any case art is treated as *therapy* for the artist and a rash of symptoms to the doctor. The doctor, bless him, can explain just what was wrong with any of the old masters.

Living artists, meanwhile, feeling misunderstood, sometimes welcome the psychologist's picture of the sick, half-mad genius. They help foist it upon the world. And the world loves the illusion that people who are "different" must also be in a bad way. A handful of painters who seem to fit the pattern—Toulouse-Lautrec, Van Gogh, Modigliani—are made ikons of distress. Press and film are brought to bear, and the lie grows.

To pity is mostly adding insult to injury. The truth is that great artists in particular are healthier, more at peace and wiser than the run of men. Their cup runneth over; hence their art. This applies even to so "tragic" a master as Van Gogh. His pictures show, and his letters document the fact, that he painted in blissful communion with reality. By superhuman effort he shaped from his bliss—and practically from that alone—a style as personal, compelling and direct as any the world has known. Of course, the pendulum kept swinging back from this tremendous work —which dizzied him and eventually drove him out of his mind. The fact remains that as an artist Van Gogh was the opposite of insane: he was more than sane.

The chance to *swagger* is what motivates policemen, doormen, even statesmen. It is not absent from art either. As a motivating factor, it lies somewhere between the taste for glory and the horror of frustration. Apart from that, the usefulness of swagger is appalling. Swagger gets publicity; and publicity, as Gertrude Stein shrewdly noted, beats literature. Publicity beats art as well. It has turned a host of artists into profitable public personalities. One sometimes mistakes the personality for the painter.

What is personality? Everything one does will express it. Even in so exacting a discipline as baseball, for example, how differently do Ted Williams and Stan Musial stand up to the plate! The first swings like a crusader surrounded; the second like a pigmy ambushing a crane. In contemporaneous books with the same setting—Melville's passionately metaphysical *Confidence Man* and Mark Twain's worldly, humorous *Life on the Mississippi*—the titans of American literature expressed diametrically opposed personalities. Yet Musial and Williams, Melville and Twain, are more pairs than opposites. So personality, for all its power, is not the main thing about a man. Personality is rather an emanation of that hollow reed, the "I."

The "I" might be compared to the mast of a great ship showing above the horizon. Or it might be compared to a watchtower, a billboard, a sideboard—to almost anything except a whole man. "I" invariably misrepresents the infinite, and any single human being is infinite.

Therefore, children avoid, as long as they possibly can, saying "I" at all.

Consider that wife-abandoning lady-killer, consummate swaggerer and prince of personality-projectors, Paul Gauguin. His "I" was bluff, tough, adventurous, proud. By contrast his art is gentle as a girl receiving first communion, cool as a sarong and calm as a cup of coconut milk. His wild egotistical dreams Gauguin lived. His paintings he appears to have dreamt. They represent that place on the far side of personality, over the horizon, where the rainbow pours out.

Works of art that conform to the artist's personality, like a life-mask to the face, are worthless. Life-masks always look like death-masks, and neither one shows character. All great art does show character—often running counter to personality, as in Gauguin's case. And character comes clearest where the artist is least concerned with self-expression.

Velásquez' court portraits at the Prado, especially the portraits of dwarfs, make this clear. The artist chose to remove himself absolutely, in favor of his sitters. He made each one represent humanity, as a misshapen little knot of our common ligaments, nerves and blood. Yet each of his dwarfs is terribly a self. Wetting and drawing tight an especially frayed, tortured knot, Velásquez shoves it under the viewer's nose, shakes it in his face. These people, he shouts, are alive! One can hardly believe that they are really dead or that the painter himself is long since dead, and all the stuff of this compassion so much dust. It might almost be easier to believe in one's own death.

Turning from the portraits one feels as if he were turning from life itself. For without knowing it he has been standing in Velásquez' place, looking through long-dead eyes and through the eye of imagination, which is eternal.

By removing himself from his work, Velásquez still causes others to become Velásquez. Never did any artist less willingly or more profoundly impress himself upon mankind.

For every artist who craves to swagger and express himself there is another who desires only to stay still somewhere and *to belong*. Stealing into history, he sits down in a corner with his sketchbook.

Left alone, he may do very well. But the makers of history, looking to their own honor, are forever urging him to commemorate historical occasions. They suppose that pictures can recapture great events—many happy returns of the day. When painters go along with this the results are generally foolish: dumb shows in costume. In historical pictures, as Mark Twain observed, "a good legible label is usually worth, for information, a ton of significant attitude and expression."

Where deliberate efforts fail, devoted ones succeed. The artists who embody history are those who fall in love with their own time and place. Greenwich Village had its John Sloan. A Paris night club found its dark little angel in Toulouse-Lautrec. Passing to the sublime, El Greco's *View of Toledo* at the Metropolitan is much more than a view. It is a vision both of and by Toledo, because El Greco, immigrant, became the very spirit of the city. In fact he still hovers there, over the shouting of lottery vendors and the sparkle of Toledo steel paper knives.

Of artists' motivations, that completes the usual list: money, power, glory, love, therapy, a chance to swagger, and a sense of place. Since each of these applies to many other callings, none by itself can be a sufficient reason for choosing art above all. Does some special constellation of them make an artist?

It may be so, in the sense that certain alloys in the right proportions make false gold. But false gold tarnishes. Pure gold is pure first of all, and one has the same feeling about the great masters.

The motivations of a minor artist, then, may well be self-centered and multifold, but art at its height requires a further motivation, independent of the ones already given. This driving force, this yearning, will be common to all great artists and to some splendid failures as well, since desire is never enough. And just as it is independent of lesser motivations so will it be free of historical circumstances, appearing when and where it will—in Borneo, Byzantium or even Boston. It will attain full strength in the artist's maturity, as lesser motivations fall away. And it will make him press forward to create in the very jaws of death.

What is this magic yearning? Perhaps the question should be put another way. Genius presumably does what it wants to do; it fulfills desire. What is it, then, that a great artist does? What is he always doing?

He repeats himself, with improvements.

Spiritual slaves do not repeat themselves, or else repeat themselves exactly. The free man grows by means of repetitions with improvements. This is surpassingly true of the freest among men, the great creative artist. The force of his desire lies in the fact that with him, yearning, struggle and reward all interlock continuously. The chains of his yearning are themselves his strength, and conductors of his light.

By their fruits, each harvest-time, ye shall know them. Through creative repetition the artist knows and improves himself. By providing its own repeated tests of spiritual growth, art hastens and guides that growth.

Art is bread upon the waters, and it nourishes what is best in the giver. To cast one's bread upon the waters, again and again, farther and farther out into the storm, and welcome it again in peace of spirit, and renew the struggle—such is the true artist's whole yearning and reward.

Since evolution itself proceeds by the same means—repetition with improvements—artists may be called the pioneers of conscious human evolution. They are heroes. Was not Homer a greater hero than Hector, let alone lipless Achilles? He was a hero born not to slaughter other heroes but to create them, and to give them immortality. His created heroes show the astonishing size of what a man may feel and do. Thus they create new heroes in life. Homer, just as much as Aristotle, was Alexander's teacher.

Heracles and Homer's heroes were the models Alexander set himself to imitate and live up to—not monkey-fashion but with free manly reverence and ambition both. All men of inner quality have practiced a similar self-modeling: sometimes on real heroes, sometimes on created ones and sometimes on both combined. Only by such free imitation, repeated to the breaking-point, can a man radically improve himself. There can be no true freedom without self-control, and no true self-control without discipline and no true discipline without imitation and no true imitation without repetition. One is so lucky, therefore, that the sun keeps on rising!

One is better inside for knowing Homer and one is better inside for knowing what remains of Greek sculpture. The reason is the same: one imitates and goes on imitating

—whether much or little, consciously or unconsciously—what one finds in each. Great art keeps inviting man to practice freedom through imitation. Self-controlled freedom, that is: aimed freedom. The best statues of Buddha, for example, invite one to contemplate just as he does, and through contemplation to follow him. The invitation is there each time.

Such creative heroes as Van Gogh or Velásquez are constant models for mankind through their art. Each time an artist of stature repeats himself with improvements he builds another step in his own evolution—a solid step, that others may climb.

This is the artist's purpose, and his place in human evolution as a whole.

Chapter 5

Sculpture into Spirit

MICHELANGELO'S "DAVID" HAS OVERLARGE HANDS, feet and head. This helps to dramatize his gawky, proud, fierce youthfulness—spirit swelling the lean pale flesh. *David* is heroic youth carved by heroic youth. Partly by his choice of subject did young Michelangelo achieve that wonderful and wild contradiction: an immature masterpiece.

When the gigantic block of marble first came into Michelangelo's hands it had already been carved at and botched by someone else. So he had to work within a troublesome and confining shape of the stone. Therefore the constraint of *David's* pose results partly from a technical problem. But it is also the constraint of youth. *David* will raise those great murderous marble hands to change the course of history. Michelangelo lifts and lets fall his own huge, hot, knotted hands to mold human spirit.

The figure has got to be gigantic. *David* is looking for invisible Goliath, far above one's head. *David's* own painful frown reflects the wound he will inflict on Goliath's brow. Invisible, vast Goliath is much older than he, and this huge youth in turn seems after all to be much older than oneself. It is a matter of generations. One gets a child's-eye view.

Even more than Michelangelo's were Greek sculptures intended as models for mankind. The whole point about Greek sculpture is that it was meant to be imitated, not in stone but in flesh. This is what imparts its miraculous life: a life so intense that even an armless, legless, headless Greek marble of the best quality shows where the head and limbs would be, upon the air. From the torso one can strike the stance of the entire figure. The broken statue seems more alive than one's own flesh. This can give rise to shame at one's own lethargy, combined with pride in the shaping spirit of mankind and, finally, an urge to godliness—as was intended.

The maimed do not enter heaven: the spiritually maimed, that is.

The monumental bronze *Charioteer* at Delphi rides out of archaic Greece like a vision of the future. It is hard to see that this is just a fragment, although one arm is missing and from the remaining hand ray broken reins. Once there were horses, actually, and the pedestal was once a chariot. But the essence of all this remains in the *Charioteer*. He is so still at the center—this youth rounding the corner of an ancient, ancient race—he is so still, so perfect in his vertical balancing calm, so self-contained, like a fountain, that all is taken up in him and balanced and released again.

Socrates evoked the Real in the Ideal and the Ideal in the Real. Strangely enough, this power left Greek sculpture long before it entered Greek philosophy. Art will keep falling away, into mere idealism on the one hand or mere realism on the other. When beauty is made an ideal in itself and separated off from the fullness of life it becomes the bathing-beauty sort, ever more vapid. Thus the late-classical Greek gods have more dimples than divinity. When, on the contrary, faithful realism becomes the criterion, separated off from spirit as the slave is from his freedom, sour slavishness results. Thus the Roman school of portraiture substituted warts for dimples and blind, grim-lipped character for the divine in man.

Only imagination—that eternal youth—can yoke the Ideal and the Real together to his chariot. Whether in philosophy or art, this is the triumph of imaginative vision.

Heracles, the best man that Zeus ever sired, was not only as strong as an oak but also passionate and wise. Commissioned to steal the apples of the Hesperides, he had the good sense to inveigle Atlas into performing the actual theft. While Atlas was about it, Heracles held up the heavens in his place. Not until Saint Christopher's time was any mere man to bear such a heavy load again.

By holding the stars upon his head, Heracles gained the apples of immortality. And it is true that a sense of eternity —if not immortality—will often spring from contemplating ageless powers: stars, mountains, oceans, man.

Atlas, glad to be relieved of the heavens' weight, offered to carry the golden apples back to Greece, if only Heracles would stand in for him meanwhile. Craftily the hero agreed: "Just take the load a minute while I find a cushion to put between the heavens and my head." Atlas consented and Heracles marched off whistling, tossing the apples in his hand. They were returned, however. One does not bring a vision home to keep.

The capitals of the Temple of Poseidon at Corinth are like cushions inserted between column and pediment, or between Heracles and the heavens. From the building of that temple to the Parthenon the Greeks gradually pared their Doric capitals from a soft round line to a tense out-springing one. This took time because they were conservative craftsmen in marble and they could not be sure how far the paring process ought to go. Similarly Frank Lloyd Wright has pushed his reinforced concrete cantilevers farther and farther out over the years. Ideas such as the cantilever and the Doric capital take shape slowly in and through the appropriate materials. Yet when a shape attains perfection it seems almost immaterial.

The Parthenon is not marble so much as idea. It shows how true, alive and balanced thought can be. It was not shaped to measure but to measured thought. This by the way is also what distinguishes Brancusi's *Bird in Space* from a propeller blade.

To make their capitals like thoughtful heads channeling the weight of worlds above, the Greeks shaped them smaller, tenser than before. Thought has no bulk. And people are apt to think of their own heads as being smaller than the actuality. Also their hands and feet and especially their genitals appear smaller to themselves than they do to others. In fact other people see these same parts larger than the actuality, because these are the more expressive parts: they tell about the person.

For the sake of power and expressiveness most sculpture, especially the primitive, exaggerates the head, hands, feet and genitals. African idols, for example, with their huge heads and eyes, embody spirits. To admire them merely as cold forms is patronizing. The same is true of Epstein's sculptures. Rodin also tended to exaggerate the expressive parts of the body. But he vacillated, and when students admired the feet of one of his figures he smashed the feet. "But," cried his apprentice, "they were the best part!" "Exactly," said Rodin. Picasso in his classicizing period also emphasized the expressive parts, which is anything but classical. The Greeks made them smaller than the actual, as they appear subjectively.

The Parthenon capitals are subjective abstractions of the human head. Instead of cushioning a weight they channel it, like thought. The column is the body, treelike and also manlike, firmly standing. It brings the strength of the ground up through the capital to meet the pediment, where the gods live, and it brings the weight of the pediment down through the capital to bedrock.

To see the ruins of the Parthenon is to see Greek thought. And the ruins are enough. It is as if the missing stones had passed not into thin air but into human consciousness.

As Zeus once ruled on Mount Olympus, so an early classical bronze of him now rules the Archeological Museum at Athens. Some say that the naked, life-size figure really represents Poseidon, and that it once brandished a trident. The statue was found in the sea. Still, its terrible grandeur calls the Father of the Gods irresistibly to mind. Light as a cloud, fine as fine rain, forceful as an avalanche, he strides. His bare, narrow feet seem gliding over the ground. In fact one foot hardly touches; he could wheel in a flash.

The calf and thigh muscles tense with life. Life pulses in the hollows back of the knees, the tight scrotum and dartlike phallus. The Greeks believed that the center of individual life lay not in the heart or head, but in the liver. Hence, perhaps, the exaggerated muscles over Zeus' narrow hips. The torso breathes life; the soul was air, according to the Greeks. The bearded head is impassive, and radiant. The left hand stretches straight out, taking aim; the narrow finger tips tremble upon the air. The right hand is cocked back, balancing and ready to hurl an invisible thunderbolt.

Here is God made in man's image. He shows how magnificent man can be. Circling the statue one straightens and breathes deeper, happily aware of one's own body, almost feeling the blood in one's own veins. Passing before the aim of that outstretched left hand, one experiences a thrill of fear. The god can kill, and he will, inexorably. Death comes from another world than ours.

That moment passes. It will never be forgotten, however, no more so than the other moments when death came close. Shaken, circling to the side of the god, one takes comfort from him. It is good to be on his good side. One hesitates, humbly, and then—why not?—strikes the same stance: striding, taking aim, thunderbolt balanced aloft. Ah! Man, too, is a death-dealer! No, but that does not altogether satisfy. Zeus was no mere death-dealer. What else did his thunderbolt bring? Fire! Inspiration! Zeus keeps sending fire into the world, by lightning. "Male lightning," the Navajo Indians call it. Their "female lightning" is heat lightning, the wide soft flash at the horizon. Male lightning is the thunderbolt of Zeus, a common cause of death in Navajo country, not in Greece. In Greece it was more of a sign and a wonder. It stopped time still; it violated Mother Earth.

Zeus had done these things in actuality. When he vanquished his cannibalistic father, Cronus, he stopped time. By insatiably seducing the daughters of Mother Earth, he violated Her. Zeus offends moralizing minds. Therefore he has slowly diminished, in civilized thought, to become a symbol of the petty tyrant: lecherous, murderous, unbright. But the ancients worshiped him above all, and they revered his acts. Why?

The Cretans maintained that Zeus is born, dies and is buried anew every year in a cave. "Cretans," said a problematic Cretan, "are liars." In truth "Zeus" was a title taken by the priest-kings of Crete, who reigned for one year and were then sacrificed to the "Great Goddess." This Great Goddess has in her myriad forms embraced the world. She has been the Navajo "Spider Woman" and the Celtic "Tree Mother." She has been the Cabalists' "Earth" and "Air," as in the red gown and blue cloak of the Madonna. She has been the "Tao" of China. She has been the "Jaguar" of stone-age Mexico—a jaguar with forests for spots, who feeds and finally devours her own young.

So men have always snuggled up to the Great Goddess, knowing she will kill them. Death is a sleep, a going to sleep in her lap. The beauty of her religion and ritual, in Crete as elsewhere, lay in helping to reconcile man to the life-cycle. They knew themselves born, loved and destroyed of the Goddess, and also resurrected in new forms. For she was in herself both space and time, bringing all things into life and out of it again and again forever. Until Zeus —not the Cretan priest but the Greek god Zeus—dared laugh at the Goddess and overturn her ritual. He demanded, not comfort, but eternity, eternity for himself and his family and even for some few men as well. Now the Greek sons of Zeus preferred his lightning bolts of courage to all the hopeless comfort, the milky mortal round, offered by the Goddess. And by this preference they determined ours.

Bold Zeus, by stopping time and violating space, showed our way. He set the face of man toward eternity. He deals not death alone but also eternity. And to imitate the statue of Zeus in dealing eternity may be to understand what one is doing all the time. It can illuminate like a lightning bolt the darkness of conscious life.

One knows and does not know that what is done is meant, is intended by the doer, and cannot be undone. One thinks to blink the truth away and to pretend that one cannot help what one does, that the responsibility lies elsewhere. "God," says the badly brought-up child, "gave me a runny nose." Then Zeus comes with his thunderbolts. Be courageous, he says, as you created me. I am Zeus, conqueror of space and time, and Father of the Gods; look at me! I am yourself!

What each person does, at each moment, he does by choice. Hard choice it may be, a choice of horrors, perhaps, or of blessings. Still, it is his choice, and cannot be undone, not for all eternity. It is done; he did it. There is ecstasy in this. Watch a child about to throw a toy out of its crib; how his face lights up! Already, he is practicing finality. The same with Zeus and his thunderbolt. The same with all of us. We know our fate is of each moment, we know it is eternal, and we know what it is. Ever since classical times we have known what man's fate is. We have known it in our hearts and we have acted upon it.

Man's fate is to be free.

Chapter 6

What Do Artists See?

WHEN HE WAS A CHILD BENVENUTO CELLINI SAW a salamander dancing in the flames upon his father's hearth. This was a sign of great good fortune and to help the boy remember it, his father struck him.

Earth has its serpent and bear; Air has the lifted birds, and Water the shining fish. Only Fire, of the four elements, lacks a living animal at its heart. Therefore one had to be invented. Cellini saw the salamander with the eye of imagination, but he really did see it. And anyone who really sees a salamander is blessed with childlike faith of the kind that makes an artist.

The kind of faith one feels in stepping aboard an elevator is comparable to faith in magic; it is cold. Instead of leading through surprise to wisdom it takes the low road through predictability to knowledge. At its best, this dull, essential faith has inspired "the black arts" of ancient times, and also "scientific miracles." Only creative art is beyond its powers.

The kind of faith essential to creative art compares with the child's faith in dolls. Warm and lively is this kind of faith! What spirit, wisdom and personality the child confers upon a favorite doll! Let that doll be common, tasteless, dirty, hairless, broken, ragged, half the paint sucked off . . . no matter. The child long ago ceased to observe it as a physical thing. Holding the little wreck in his arms, he sees with the eye of imagination a soulmate or an angel. If he can only keep this power of faith, the child may grow up to envision, like Michelangelo, a David in a block of marble.

What has art to do with dolls and salamanders? It has to do with everything. To limit the study of art to art alone is playing it safe—like the ostrich. One suffocates. Or rather, one dies to the world of imagination. Everything flows into imagination and thence into art. So the best way to understand art is to participate imaginatively in its sources. To study art should be to study life imaginatively. No one ever carved or painted a masterpiece except in the light of imagination. The great artists are all visionaries; seeing their work is like seeing visions.

No one before Raphael saw the Umbrian plain as he saw it. No one before Goya saw the Spanish people as they have ever since remained. For eons *Mont Saint Victoire* awaited Cézanne's genius, as the cypresses around Arles awaited the coming of Van Gogh. Did these men paint these things just as they really are? "Yes!" the traveler exclaims, spreading his arms. But no: he sees what the masters saw, fused with what they envisioned. Taught by their pictures he himself stands gazing, rapt, through the eye of imagination.

Every great painting shows something seen plus something seen into: it brings sight and insight together.

Without imaginative insight, the artist just paints surfaces. His pictures may be brilliant, flawless, charged with wild emotion; they may win the highest praise but they will still be surface painting. Likewise the man who looks at painting unimaginatively will see only surfaces—even with a masterpiece before him. And the more he studies the surface the less he will understand what is within.

Even the most powerful imagination sometimes fails to penetrate a masterpiece. A great portrait, for example, will reveal itself only to one who understands his fellows. Mark Twain said that he especially enjoyed meeting in novels people whom he had "already met on the River."

To a child, Titian's *Duke Frederick of Saxony,* at the Prado, will seem an ogre. To the student, he will appear a most ungentle knight. But imaginative insight coupled with personal experience may penetrate, as Titian himself did, through the lobster-shell of black armor and the hill of scarred burly flesh encased therein, to the invisible, where a dauntless, melancholy soul stands pinned.

At a certain pitch of imaginative recollection, material clues no longer matter. Velásquez' portraits of the court dwarfs at Madrid, or Goya's dream-figures from the "House of the Deaf Man," stand outside of common physical experience, and yet they seem overwhelmingly familiar. They are like the disembodied souls of people one has known and failed. Such art seems close to sorcery but it is not.

Genius can be explored a little way, which helps it grow and spread to other men. The genius never wears a sorcerer's cap, though sometimes a minor artist claps one on.

Far out towards the horizon, the Mediterranean Sea deepens to Tyrian purple—a color that ancient kings and emperors reserved for their own robes. Thus the lords of the earth thought to put a distance between themselves and other men. But now it is a few minor artists who use lordliness. Through their boasts, art dims. There is, for example, a superstition, gleefully indulged by some painters, that artists "see differently" from other men. From this comes the further fallacy that a painter's private vision may be incomprehensible to all ordinary men and yet immortal in itself.

Some years ago a sober-sided fact-finder buttonholed a young prince of the abstract-expressionist camp: "When I look at the ocean I see that it is wet and green. What do you see?" Without a smile the painter replied: "I see atomic particles." He lied of course.

Yet the fact-finder also was in error. Nobody "sees" that the ocean is wet. Looking at it, one imagines that.

Recently an abstraction called *The Sea* came before a museum purchasing committee. "I've had a yacht for sixty years," growled the chairman, "and I never saw the sea looking like that!"

The problem is an old one. An English critic once complained that he had never seen a sunset like those painted by Whistler. "Ah?" rejoined the great-uncle of modern art. "Don't you wish you had!"

Physically, one man sees very like another. The physical eyes can hardly be trained, though glasses help. But the eye of imagination can be trained. In great men it supplements and sometimes even dominates the physical eyes. Some would call that "clairvoyance" but there is no need to make it so mysterious. The astrologer who says that he can look right through the blue blaze of noon to see the stars beyond, lies. Yet the astronomer can, with a glance at his watch, accurately picture their position from where he stands. "Clairvoyance" is disciplined imagination—imagination shaped to hidden truths.

Imagination, that most general and human of powers, is also the artist's special faculty. The marvelous depth and variety of artists' ways of seeing have no stranger cause than this. Moreover, the physical eyes and the eye of imagination can only work together in the artist; neither excludes the other.

A favorite discipline of certain artists is to see nature herself as a work of art. When already an old man, with a long career of conscientious picture-making behind him, Maurice Sterne experienced this discipline and was reborn into the creative realm. It happened this way: he was resting, convalescing, on his porch at Cape Cod, gazing out over the wind-roiled, green and white Atlantic Ocean, when suddenly a sea gull swooped into view. "The fool," Sterne thought. "He'll get his wings all smeared with paint!"

Sterne's best canvases stem from this experience. They give the other side of it. Since he came at last to experience nature as painting, one experiences his last paintings as nature. Of course the sea gull is their least convincing element. All the rest appears to be dissolving outwards, towards one, in gusts of summer storm off the salt sea.

Painting dissolves the forms at its command, or tends to; it melts them into color. Drawing, on the other hand, goes about resolving forms, giving edge and also essence to things. To see shapes clearly, one outlines them—whether on paper or in the mind. Therefore, Michelangelo, a profoundly cultivated man, called drawing the basis of all knowledge whatsoever.

To rob children of this basis is little short of criminal. They should be taught to draw. Not only that but plied with drawings, and the eyes of their imaginations nourished thereby. This nourishment should not include too many comic-book potato chips. Nor should it lean to cartoons of the Walt Disney sort, which boil the hardness of rocks, the rootedness of plants, the animality of animals and indeed the vigor of all nature down to marzipan. Nor, finally, should "realistic" drawing of the Norman Rockwell kind be given too much place. Growing children hunger for drawings that show what their eyes can see and also what their minds can see—both together, as in nature. Real drawing, in short. And fortunately there are still a few, a very few, children's books illustrated in the real way.

Imagine a precisely realistic illustration to Baron Munchausen's story about a horse leaping broadside through the windows of a coach: could it possibly convince? Gustave Doré was able to add conviction to Munchausen's charm. His drawing imperceptibly slims and elongates the horse and lifts its legs straight out and makes it sail through those coach windows as naturally as an arrow.

Doré was in a class by himself in France. England has had half a dozen illustrators of his caliber. Cruikshank, Tenniel, Shepard, the writer-artists Thackeray and Lear, all were masters not of realism but of realization. They were literary, not literal, forming visions out of words. The problem of making their visions look "real," as factual as can be, was always secondary and comparatively simple.

E. H. Shepard's *Pooh* is real, not realistic. Can one imagine *Pooh* drawn by somebody else? He lives in and through Shepard's drawings. Would it seem extravagant to say that Shepard drew him and not pictures of him at all? Or to wonder if these drawings may not well outlive Graham Sutherland's thorn trees and Francis Bacon's lavender cardinals?

Certainly Tenniel shows no signs of fading. Later illustrations to Lewis Carroll are just pictures; his remain the truth. He could define for all time even so soupy a character as the Mock Turtle, and when he confessed that he failed to "see" a wasp in a bonnet—one of the original cast of *Through the Looking Glass*—Carroll realistically cut her out of the story.

Tenniel was great; he did immense good in the world. What then is one to say about those draftsmen of genius who illustrate not books but life itself with infinitely greater clarity—such as Blake, for example, and the diamond-souled Dürer?

Before touching pen to paper, Dürer saw his drawings clear. They have the truth, economy and balance of mathematical equations. Also they vibrate with feeling. Far from coldly tracing his visions, Dürer encouraged his hand to dance with and embellish them. Indeed the dance of his hand is so beautiful it disappears. Try as one may to follow the turns, cuts, falls, folds, leaps and gatherings made by Dürer's lines, one sees instead a vision. There his genius lies.

Drawing without first visualizing is a dance in the dark. To visualize as clearly and powerfully as Dürer did brings light into the world. He drew by his own light. To sense the miracle one need only try to project an original drawing such as Dürer's in imagination upon a blank page.

Modestly and frugally Dürer made a habit of drawing on both sides of the paper. Yet he did once note with something like surprise that a ten-minute sketch of his could carry more conviction than some other fellow's ten-year struggle.

Dürer drew everything, from the sun right down to *A Small Piece of Turf*. Universality is what distinguishes genius from talent. That, and the full power to imagine. As fantasy is to real imagining, so decoration is to masterpieces. Fantasy and decoration play along the edges of things. Imagination plunges within, seeking essence.

Why do distant objects appear small? Because they are distant. The bodily senses sift the truth into patterns relating to the body, which is busy with the near-at-hand. Thus the body both informs and frees the mind, which roams at will. For example, the mind understands that those inch-high poplars along the far stream are really tall and shady within. It goes over, so to speak, and checks.

Closing one's eyes while standing on one foot gives an effect of motion, for the mind is tightrope walking. On a high cliff one holds onto something, for fear of following one's own gaze down into the abyss. Sometimes a path of moonlight on the water looks solid enough to walk on, like floating gold ingots. This is partly an effect of perspective: the mind walks in confidence because the path is plain.

This is just as true in pictures as in nature. One's mind enters both alike, as an invisible and yet perfectly real being. In fact the space-making power of pictures is that they first show something to the eye and then invite the mind to enter it. One is involved as in nature.

So great is the space-making power of pictures that even a mere diagram may have some of it. Imagine three straight lines arranged to indicate a road converging at a horizon. Either one sees only the pattern or else one is walking down that road.

The truth about the diagram is a thousand times more true in a Cézanne, for example. Therefore it does seem wrong to consider pictures as mere objects, inert. In space-making terms alone they are dynamic forces. The masterpieces are like great trains at the station, or airplanes revving up, ready to take one aboard. Or they are generators softly humming, throbbing, generating.

Chinese legend tells of a painter who opened a little door in his own mural, entered, and closed the door behind him. It was never found, nor was the painter seen again.

Chinese art brings space alive in a cloudy, writhing, rhythmic way. To enter it imaginatively is rather like stepping onto a dance floor in the moonlight. Cézanne's landscapes on the other hand are huge, regardless of their actual size, and still as noon and thousand-faceted and filled to brimming with the Mediterranean sun. One can live within them by the hour. In fact one feels that one might pass around the curve of a road in a Cézanne and disappear, yet still be there, beyond, within the picture.

Imagination in its glory plays between the subject and object. It partakes of the mind, whose nature is to abstract freely, and also of objects, which are concrete. Therefore great works of imagination can be free, abstract and yet objective—specific every time.

Generalizations may be drawn from art, but never the reverse. Just as the criminal hates laws and the philosopher hates inconsistencies, so the true artist abominates all generalizations. The painter of picture post-cards or calendar girls generalizes, but he is not an artist. Nor is the painter of perfunctory dining-room still lifes. "Fruit," *per se,* never made a work of art. Cézanne therefore painted real apples, particular apples, and not types or symbols or "pure forms" either. Yet with all this he was a shaper more than anything, a sculptor of the air. Reality, that was Cézanne's test.

And yet Poussin was his model. Poussin had best loved arranging shapes—especially the shapes of hills, trees, columns, clouds, and river valleys—until they locked and balanced perfectly in space. It was not his concern to imitate the real thing very closely: just enough for a polite illusion, as in charades. He was a studio-painter, not an outdoor man. His landscapes are like scenery within which classic figures pose: *Diana and Actaeon* or suchlike. The figures carry small conviction but the settings are splendid. Simply as arrangements of shapes in space, Poussin's canvases inspire the imagination to stroll, fly, swim, caress. This quality Cézanne adored. He saw that the illustrative element might be removed without loss, however, and sunshine introduced. He took away the theatre.

From his impressionist friends Cézanne had learned the one truth necessary to complete Poussin. It was that the illusion of reality can be immensely reinforced when one takes the trouble to paint on the spot. Then abstract loveliness will wear its natural dress. This is what Cézanne meant when he said that his ambition was "to do Poussin over again from nature." Far more than any impressionist, though, Cézanne saw the forms within the dress. He had no need to invent them, like Poussin, for they were there. His imagination raced and pressed amongst the real.

There are no "pure forms." Nothing that is seen at all can be totally without significance. Physical vision requires mind as well as eye, subject as well as object. Moreover, it requires a certain separation, a distance. Picasso's three-eyed girls may sometimes represent a mistress seen too close, yet even here there is a little distance still. A thing put right against the eyeball is invisible.

The image of the seen must leap across a void to the eye. Vision also makes the leap, in the opposite direction. The eye is not a passive, cheap receiving set but itself a shaping instrument. Seeing is a power, projected outwards from the center of a man. If it does not seem so, one has only to ask a blind man—or to close one's own eyes. Is the desire to re-open them like wanting to let in the light? Or is it not more like wanting to step out of doors? Through sight, the mind steps out of doors.

By staring hard at someone who is both oblivious and some distance away, one can often make him turn and meet one's eyes. In fact this works with practically everybody except waiters—who have been immunized. Some weird explanations for this every-day phenomenon have been offered, but the most obvious explanation is that seeing is an active power and not just a passive one. It is a projection of the seer, which the person being looked at can actually feel.

If this be true of physical vision, how still more true it is of the eye of imagination! Imagination leaps and flows and forms at will upon the void that separates the seer from the seen. This world between the worlds, between subject and object, is imagination's natural realm. Also, it is where great artists roam at will, on rainbow dragons of the air.

Still there is no sorcery about the way these masters work. In them the eye of imagination has developed its natural power to fabulous proportions; that is all. Every man possesses the eye of imagination to start with, and almost everyone can develop it further—most especially through art.

"When a woman combs her hair," said Rodin, "she imitates the motions of the stars."

That is creative seeing.

Chapter 7

New Maps for Old Treasure

THOSE WITH A DESIRE TO EXPLORE THE HIDDEN realms of art find plenty of maps provided. The question, as with all treasure-maps, is whether or not they prove useful.

The maps to art fall under certain categories of seeing. For example, the maps of the experts are based on scholarly, authoritative seeing. The critics' maps are based on judgments—critical seeing. The materialists' maps are based solely on what the physical eyes can see. The aestheticians' maps are based on a cool, theoretical sort of seeing. All these are useful. But a still better way to the treasure lies through personal, imaginative vision. And for this new maps are needed.

The expert doctor specializing in gall bladders can tell at a glance whether to operate or to pass his patient on to a crony in cardiac conditions or gastric ulcers. If he bothers to X-ray it is probably for the sake of form. Similarly, the baseball scout knows whether or not a certain high-school long-ball-hitter is Big League material. He is not paid to guess; he knows. In the field of art also such feats of "expertise" are commonplace. One man authenticates archaic bronzes at a glance. Another can tell Cree from Tlingit-ware. A third finds evidence of alien hands in almost every single Giorgione. A fourth dates Dresden china to the decade. How are these things done?

The trick is simply to learn all the facts about a given branch of art, and to store its known examples as images in one's mind. Then one tests problematic works against those facts and images. It is very like comparing fingerprints, and just as quick. Speed is characteristic, in fact, of expertise in all professions. The labor came before, in the learning. The instantaneous application of that learning produces an effect of sorcery, but it is really second-nature.

Yet to express a personal opinion on a work of art brings chills and fever to the well-stuffed head. When it comes to publishing his findings, the art expert turns as hesitant as he was quick before. One mistake can ruin a reputation, and he knows his colleagues will be politely merciless. This is why so much art scholarship seems bold and free to those involved and stiff-collared to others.

Dealers must sometimes be experts in a dozen or more branches of art. Also their business requires quick decisions and quick turnover. They too are often conservatives, however.

Imagine a connoisseur of wine, a millionaire of course, trying to sort out the master-bottles by taste alone, without expert help. He could be drunk all his life and still have made only a start. Once enjoyed, the wine is gone forever. Art remains, and in itself corrects the judgments of authority. This takes time: close to a hundred years. Yet clearly one can trust time-proven judgments on the old masters' best-known works. To despise the *Mona Lisa* would be silly.

Still, it is an open secret that many museums, even great ones, present inferior and occasionally spurious works as masterpieces. This comes partly from honest error, partly from local pride. It plays havoc with students, who suppose that they have seen, seen through and rejected a certain master, after having studied only an imitation. There may even have been a real example, a sketch that one missed, tucked away in the gloom of a corridor.

It pays to pay attention to authority, and then to keep wondering—not doubting, exactly, but wondering.

There was once in San Francisco a blind dealer in Chinese jade, who bought and sold the rarest pieces by touch alone. Similarly, the most brilliant, reliable and renowned of experts may be totally blind to art itself. Art has no provenance or price-tag; art is an event—an event in the hearts and minds of those who really see what they are looking at. The expert does not concern himself with this. Indeed, he cannot even allow himself to be moved. Emotion would obscure his real concern: style, which can be classified. He sees not the seed, but the husk. This ought not to be a cause for complaint. The expert keeps art in order, more or less, guarding its gates and kinds and hierarchies and introducing people to these things. When one tips one's hat and asks for facts, he can satisfy astoundingly.

One would not go to a gall-bladder man to discover the meaning of existence, nor to a gynecologist to learn about love. Nor would one ask a certified public accountant to judge a career. Nor should one ask an art expert about things of the spirit, unless after hours.

The art expert's chief contribution can only be to save the amateur—the lover—time. By smoothing the search he saves one time for enjoyment. This means a lot because enjoyment always does take time—as much with art as with literature or music.

Masterpieces are the flowers of the field of art—as different from the rest as flowers are from grass—and one gets to the point of caring only for them. Their splendors open slowly like flowers and this is the best of experiencing art. Authority should lead one straight to the masterpieces, and then withdraw.

Sometimes in a museum one sees people sitting quietly before the pictures. The crowd nudges past them, with glances of suspicion and dislike. These people are resting their feet, no doubt. Or, just possibly, they may be waiting to comprehend something.

Everyone has had the disappointment of approaching a known masterpiece and finding it a blank, as empty of significance as a whitewashed wall. When this happens it is best to wait. The artist has built doors into that wall, which open by themselves if only one waits. Different people go through different doors, of course. They step into the picture, and look around, slowly.

In Bruegel's *Peasant Dance* at Vienna, for example, the door may be the lovers, the cross on the ground, the broken pot, or the birdlike man who is singing to the bagpiper. However one steps through, one steps into man-created time as well as space. If through the singer, one begins to hear his new song faintly—first the music of his voice and then the bagpipes. One feels the music swoop and lift like birds about the blind men's heads. One's own feet sense the thumping of the dancers' feet upon the ground.

To peer swiftly at the surfaces of pictures is a waste of time. The dirt obscures the varnish, the varnish obscures the glazes, the glazes obscure the underpainting, the underpainting obscures the canvas and the canvas hides the wall;

that is all. But if only one makes a slow-motion plunge into any masterpiece, and drifts within the picture on currents of imagination, its darkness lights up, from inside. Once this is understood there will be far less "scientific restoration"—scraping and scrubbing—of pictures.

This cruel fad calls for a digression. Time was when the butler used to re-varnish the ancestral portraits every spring, so that they retreated from the present year by year, as if sinking into some brown forest pool. But now major paintings are handed over to men in white smocks clutching scalpels and chemical swabs. These men take the view that everything in a picture ought to be clear, if possible. If a soft cheek has an edge, they want to see that edge knife-sharp. If there be fifty nailheads in a painted cask, they want to see all fifty. So they strip away the surface glazes, the final transparent coats and touches that are the painter's way of rendering atmosphere. Triumphantly they hand back an under-painting: the hard, precise, detailed study that the artist began with!

Hardly a single master has escaped intact, but Rembrandt appears to have suffered most of all, both in America and in Europe. His celebrated *Night Watch* at Amsterdam is now a *Day Watch*. Much that was hidden in this picture is now revealed, as if by limelight. The assumption is that Rembrandt could not possibly have wished to cast an obscuring or concealing shadow over any detail that he had previously taken the trouble to paint. But is this true? Certainly he was not a lazy man, nor did he paint to show off. He was in love with atmosphere: why should he not have sacrificed part of his labors, then, to atmosphere?

Behind the question of atmosphere there is another even more conclusive. Rembrandt, like all the great masters, painted not only for the physical eyes but also for the eye of imagination. And the better to reach the eye of imagination he would sometimes deliberately frustrate and bemuse the physical eyes. But in his scientifically cleaned canvases nothing is left to the imagination—which is to say that nothing much is left.

Picture cleaning probably should be confined to what can be done with a loaf of fresh white bread, decrusted, which is the gentlest of art-gum erasers.

Scientific restorers are death on pictures; aestheticians can be death on artists themselves.

Whether or not aesthetics can be called a science, it practices the cool detachment of scientific inquiry. It isolates works of art as if in a laboratory for purposes of analysis. Thus it tends to ignore the artist as a human being. Or rather, aestheticians—pale, honored guests at the feast—regard the artist as a sort of cup-bearer, as a shadowy servant who has no real connection with the wine he brings. That makes it all so much simpler—to take the cup without looking at the servant.

And it is true that one ought not to be grateful for everything. One drives one's car with barely a nod to the fellows in Detroit. But a car is just matter shaped to certain useful ideas. A work of art, on the contrary, is alive with ideas of its own. Like man himself, it is both thought and thing. A masterpiece lives and gives life out to those who see it. Like the legendary cornucopia, it remains an inexhaustible horn of plenty. But the cornucopia was a spiritual creation whence flowed material abundance, whereas a masterpiece is a material creation whence flows spiritual abundance.

Whence comes this ever-flowing spiritual life, if not from

the artist? Art lives because the artist lives within it: how else? It is his own heart beating there. Some servant!

If critics are a bit less sure and cold than aestheticians it is because their main concern has got to be contemporary art—a field wherein one finds one's own flowers, like the level bee. New judgments are by definition unproven. Therefore, critics cannot be authorities, although some will become so after death. From the artists' viewpoint, critics also can go to hell. Artists like not the critical elixir —solicitude and cruelty, in equal parts. The critic who makes judging a matter of principle—who keeps criticizing instead of trying to understand—is rather like a man with a cane, alone in the garden, decapitating weeds and flowers alike. Anything that has size or mystery about it stands in danger of him.

Criticism does give the half-wild garden of contemporary art a semblance of order. Yet something new is needed, something less like weeding and more like watering the garden. It needs less judgment and more sympathy, less criticism and more straightforward interpretation.

Homer described Achilles' shield in terms of its actual making. Some day critics may talk about art in terms of its actual effect upon themselves. When that happens they will be critics no longer, but interpreters. Hephaestus did not make Achilles' shield in a moment, nor is art interpretation a matter for swiftness. Indeed while one is with a work of art one ought simply to experience it. Afterwards one sees it again in the eye of imagination, and this image one tries to interpret.

No reproductions ought to be consulted after the fact— nor books nor documents. These things may correct lapses of memory but they would also come between the interpreter and the best that is in his mind. If the copyist who paints from reproductions is a sorry case, so too is the writer on art who works from stacks of photographs and books. No photograph can shine like memory, nor can another man's words describe one's own experience. Art is living, personal experience. Interpretation hews to that, and points the way for others.

Anyone who lives by contemplating art obviously owes an eternal debt to artists. Yet critics owe more in a personal way than do aestheticians, and interpreters owe more than critics. The man who ventures to interpret a work of art must first subordinate himself, in a spirit of wonder and gratitude, to the artist's thought. This may be one reason why interpretation of art is seldom attempted. So many intellectuals hate feeling beholden. They dread emotional intimacy. Indeed, they dread emotion.

Another argument against interpreting art is the fear of error, and the still more insidious fear of censure. Interpretations need not be proved wrong; merely to deny them is enough. And errors there will always be. Yet to crouch in the dustbin of the already-known, for fear of making some mistake, is itself a serious error.

Interpretation cannot fear small errors. It is designed for the discovery of larger truths.

And yet the interpreter of art has much else to fear. The dangers of the freedom that he allows himself may be lumped in one word: deadness. His whole concern must be to transmit directly his own experience of art in a living form. Just as fresh fish is rushed from the sea to the kitchen, so should he rush his deep-sea catch into civilized converse. Canning is out.

Simply by observing a few rules of the game one may help to make art interpretation a living thing. In the first place one ought never to discuss a work of art at all unless its actuality has entered one's own consciousness. That a man who has not personally seen the Great Sphinx can interpret it is impossible.

Second, one should pass by the favorites of the iconographers—works whose symbolism is purely external and whose meanings can therefore be formulated. These indeed can be understood from reproductions alone, since their meanings are applied and not inherent. But to grasp them is to grasp mere knowledge; wisdom will be nowhere about. Merely symbolic art is in fact no art at all. The stone lions in front of the New York Public Library may serve as an example of this. They will never roar, runs an old gag, until a virgin passes by. These lions symbolize fierce majesty, no doubt, yet what they stand for is not what they are: they are inert.

Third, one ought to choose problematic works of art over those that clearly corroborate one's train of thought, to keep it from crystallizing.

Fourth, one ought to shun even the appearance of completeness. The experience of art is personal. Therefore its study should be kept conversational. To pile up evidence or fill in gaps laboriously, or justify at length, or dogmatize, kills conversation.

Fifth and finally, one ought to change the subject now and again—both for the sake of courtesy and as a discipline. The one-track mind chugs to destruction. And among the happiest attractions of art as a study is the fact that it keeps demanding shifts of viewpoint. Every masterpiece comprises a new subject. For if history is a river of blood, as the fastidious Gibbon believed, art is like a fleet of crystal ships crossing and re-crossing that river. Each vessel flies new colors with each crossing, and carries new treasure.

All art worthy of the name was alive in the making, and lives again in the seeing. This fact alone shows how peripheral are the usual questions about a work of art, questions of composition, technique, resemblance, illustration and symbolism. But when one asks a man to tell what a certain masterpiece has meant to him, then he can answer boldly, without pretension or equivocation, out of personal experience. He may not be right in what he says. Yet if the interpreter of art takes care to speak fully and honestly, from personal experience alone, he will at least be true.

Let specialists grumble and find flaws. Their maps are different, leading not to experience but to knowledgeability. The custodians of the known are not custodians of art.

Art cannot be known but only experienced. And art belongs to man.

Chapter 8

The Birth of the Invisible

IMAGINE PICTURES MADE IN UNKNOWN FASHION, BY people unknown, for unknown purposes, in times remote. Could such pictures possibly be interesting or beautiful or significant now? Cro-Magnon cave paintings, for example.

The thundering herd that shakes the cave at Altamira, and has for twenty thousand years, was painted merely to help the hunting: so say anthropologists. But anthropology falls prey, naturally, to scientific prejudice. A scientist would rather describe the cave pictures as attempts at magic than admit the fact that they appear to have been painted by magic.

Likewise the historians who maintain that the caves are historical picture books—with each tribe represented by a totem animal—are assuming that the Cro-Magnons had a passion for history to match their own.

There ought to be a third explanation for these pictures —one that takes into account their supernal splendor.

Altamira and Lascaux both hum with energy, like the dynamo rooms of great dams. So do serpentine Combarelles and Font-de-Gaume, in lesser degree. One feels that perhaps the pictures were planted here, as in the womb of Mother Earth, that beasts might multiply. Yet the animals are mostly gone from above, and some are even extinct. On the snowy slopes overhead, no yellow-eyed cave-cat will ever again be yawning at the moon.

No, these images were not made to reproduce in nature but rather in the human soul. They still do that. When the visitor sleeps the cave-cat will awaken, will come nuzzling the dark of his dream.

To remove the Sistine Chapel from its religious context would be intellectual smuggling. But Altamira has been legitimately removed from its context, or rather the context has been removed from it. Supposing that the Sistine Chapel were to be preserved alone underground for fifteen or twenty millennia, might not the anthropologists of the future mistake it for a monument of ignorance and illusion?

Altamira, too, is really a place of worship. These beasts come stampeding through the cave of one's own ribs. Possibly they did have magical or even documentary purposes; no matter: their main purpose was and is to awaken the spirit and enlighten the human soul. And this is true of all the greatest art, forever.

To see the Sistine Chapel is to know that one is Adam and that God is God. To see the Cave of the Bulls at Altamira is to feel one's own animal self surging from darkness into the firelight and on into darkness again. Michelangelo, of course, knew what he was doing. Altamira being on a similar level of mastery, one can assume that its creator also knew what he was doing.

This is not to deny the probability that both Michelangelo and the Cro-Magnon did their best work in a kind of trance. They were purposeful still; they rose consciously to heights that are beyond ordinary consciousness. And like Moses with his tablets they brought back unearthly messages. Not ignorance and superstition but knowledge and reverence prompted man to create.

The Sistine Chapel, the Medici Chapel, the School of San Rocco in Venice, the Bruegel Room at Vienna, the Acropolis, Altamira, Lascaux—all these are sacred places. Are such places "beautiful" or "interesting"? Invariably this, and how much more! The eye is not only delighted, it is overwhelmed and drowned; one weeps. And the mind within its little temple of bone is not only intrigued to find itself again entempled by such places, it is entered as if by fingers through the eyes and seized upon and violently stretched. Art and the world fall away.

After the bull-roarers of Altamira, Lascaux seems as quiet as a procession of clouds. Clearly the Cro-Magnons, like Adam in the Garden, knew the animals as brothers. These pictures show the animals to have a range of feeling such as civilized men attribute only to civilized men.

From the softly sweeping, stately and eternal passage of the animals at Lascaux there seems to come a voice, terribly afar, like the sound of goat-bells and cock-crows along a mountainside at night—a mingled voice from skies of stone. We ourselves are living, said the ancients, in a cave. The sky is of stone and the clouds are creatures.

Lascaux, then, is a microcosm of the natural vast. Also, it is interior Man.

Everything is built around nothing, like a cave. Therefore one hears silence and sees emptiness. These things flow into man, and man flows out into them. Within silence, he hears the unheard. Within emptiness, he sees the unseen. Hence the cave paintings.

There are those who complain of the "realism" at Lascaux. The history of painting, they believe, ought more reasonably to begin with indecipherable blobs; like the child with his first paint-set. And yet these earliest-known painters, they say, were clever copyists—decadent by modern standards—whose chief merit was to observe and perfectly record the curve of an animal's hoof or horn or eyelid. But the sense of reality can be conveyed by other means than copying, and so it is here. That the cave-artists' means have not been grasped, is astonishing.

Bumps and hollows in the cavern walls were incorporated in these first pictures, interchangeably. For example, a hollow would sometimes serve to reinforce the painted bulk of a bison's shoulder, or a bulge might accentuate his sucked-in belly. It was a question not of sculptured bulk, then, as in bas-relief, but of the suggestive power residing in cast shadows. And here lies the clue to the Cro-Magnon's painting method. These animals are not posing, but appearing, as in a dream. Soon one will see more coming in the stains, cracks and shadows of the cavern walls—even by flashlight. By flickering firelight or the light of animal-grease candles one would sense still more, inside the rock, creatures cloudily looming towards the world of sight.

The animals already here were swiftly pictured, often overlapping one another, by candlelight and firelight. The artists made no conscious effort to copy nor even to "convey" anything; they were capturing directly what they saw. They would put the line of a horn precisely where they saw that line already in the rock.

What they saw were shadow-pictures cast across the rough rock-face by firelight. But they saw them with the eye of imagination. What had been invisible welled up through the play of shadows. This is why so many of the creatures overlap although much nearby wall space was never filled. Design—space-filling—has nothing at all to do with the case here. Vision—infinity pressing through to the finite—has everything.

As swiftly as the visions came, the artists traced them on the walls, sometimes with firebrands, and less often with powdery pigment blown from tubes. Other visions they incised with flint, as at Combarelles and Font-de-Gaume. Many were left unfinished, as if the image had appeared only in part or else begun to fade and drift out of sight.

The famous frieze of the "swimming reindeer" at Lascaux—an arc of reindeer heads in contour—seems to leap up from the shadows and then slowly fall away as firelight would fall.

A few of the vast bulls leaping right across the ceiling at Lascaux appear to twist and billow like smoke.

These pictures show that animals blaze up within man and that man holds dominion over the animals; he is their conscious vessel as well. The animals feel their own animal natures through and through themselves, which gives them a pure beauty and completeness such as men might envy; yet only man is capable of finding and feeling and knowing and re-creating other creatures within himself.

A practical purpose for the cave paintings may have been to develop the eye of imagination along with the physical eye, and teach them to work in harmony. By candlelight and firelight the actual pictures would seem to glow forth, flicker and drift away like wraiths. Only through long practice could one see them whole, or keep them in the mind's eye. So trained, the hunter would be quick to see a real deer in a dappled wood.

The impractical, or religious purpose matters infinitely more: to carry a fructifying seed-truth into consciousness. Man sees and holds within himself both the visible and the invisible. Man can imagine. And this is the seed-truth that lights the Cro-Magnon caves. Man can see what is not there, and see it exact.

Not training but revelation is the ultimate purpose of this art: the revelation of the invisible, together with the promise made to awakening mankind that he can master even that, even the invisible.

Chapter 9

The Ark of Man and His Animals

ANIMALS RUN DEEP IN DREAMS, AND ART KEEPS leading them forth to consciousness. One might almost sketch the history of art in terms of animal subjects. Such a thread would be more down-to-earth than those of social, religious, sexual and cultural expression. Yet it also should be taken lightly. One is following a gossamer across illimitable night.

The great Assyrian bas-reliefs of lion-fights show a sport that long ago passed out of civilized consciousness. At the British Museum these reliefs form a tunnel all the way back into pre-history, where one emerges on a largely animal world.

Lion-fights may have come before bull-fights in the Middle East. At last the lion fled to Africa, where certain tribes such as the Massai still make a ritual of killing him. How to fight a lion? He leaps, and cannot much alter his course in mid-air. Also it bothers him to be pointed at, especially with pointed things. Also he may first be attacked from a distance, with arrows, and worn down.

It was common practice in Assyria to hunt and fight lions from chariots. The bas-reliefs at the British Museum show that the Assyrians were not satisfied even with this deadly sport. They chose also to fight lions more sedately, and far more dangerously, on foot in a public place. First the lion would be ringed with spears, and gradually weakened with arrows. Then they would taunt him into leaping—and missing—time after time, precisely as the Spanish matador makes the bull charge himself to exhaustion. When the lion could no longer spring, the King of Assyria stepped close, short sword in hand, a heavy mantle wrapped about his shield arm. The lion reared up to claw the mantle. The king stood firm, and drove his sword into the heart.

All this, immortal clay makes clear. There is something leonine about the ringleted king, and yet the lions are the heroes: every one a fiery reality, awesome in torment and tragic in death.

The bulls too were adored and imitated throughout the ancient world. Moreover, they were tamed. There is a pair of gold cups from a Mycenaean tomb, at the Archeological Museum in Athens, showing exactly what the bulls must have signified in the heroic age of Theseus. The bas-reliefs that ring these little cups are as tiny as the Assyrian lion-frieze is large—and equally fine. Wild bulls surround one of the cups, trampling and goring men and breaking free to plunge splendidly with huge light-footed force away and away around the little cup. The other shows the same bulls snared and tamed and yoked in harmony, their power slowed to an inexorable tread, their passion smoothed to service.

These golden, inch-high, dark, enormous beasts might be

said to represent powers outside of man; they do, yet man gave birth to the powers they possess. The artist bore those powers in himself, and then impressed them on the sunny metal.

After learning to kill animals the next great task of man was taming them. Man learned the killing lesson well, but for a long time now he has not tamed a new species. Art was an aid to both kinds of learning. It brings the tasks back again and shows that they were not only physical but also spiritual. To kill a lion one learns courage from the lion. To tame animals one learns courageously to see their shadows in oneself, making one's mind a vessel of creation, an invisible Noah's Ark.

Besides painting and sculpture there were ritual aids to all this: actual lion-fights in Assyria, bull-fights in Crete. There must have been music, too, and dancing, back to Cro-Magnon times, and bloody sacrifices. Such things come dimly through the legend of the Minotaur. If one knew the dance step one might thread the labyrinth. Ariadne's thread is memory, is consciousness. The Minotaur is man standing on his head—the brain blood-clouded like a bull's. The Minotaur is an in-between state to overcome, a human condition to conquer. Not until a man kills the Minotaur within can he stand up to Taurus.

Titian's *Rape of Europa* is the opposite of violent. This small-horned god-bull—modeled on Ovid's account—is as blue-white as skimmed milk or a June thunderhead. One round eye rolls slyly back to see his lovely burden thrill with delight and fear, as mildly he breasts the wine-dark wave.

Here Titian, that silvery sensualist, has outdone the smoothest of ancient Greeks. His Renaissance daylight hides with jovial blue the blackness of outer space. Jove's thunderbolt becomes a phallus: lightning gentles into lust.

By Goya's time the bull had ceased to be a creature formed of milk and thunderheads. It had shrunk to a mere animal. Meanwhile, its horns had sharpened—naturally. In the bull ring, it fought as if its death depended on it: a single animal at war with all the coldest, cruelest, smartest and most elusive of creatures. Robbed of significance, its sacrifice made meaningless, the bull in Goya's art is more than ever itself.

What is a bull's favorite color? Blood-red, still and forever.

The *Crowning with Thorns* by Bosch, at the National Gallery in London, makes animals of Christ's tormentors. Christ is the only human being.

Tintoretto's *Washing of the Feet,* at the Prado, has a white hound prone in the foreground. One loves the dog on sight. Later one sees Christ nearby, and afterwards the scene's significance. But why the dog? This troubled the Inquisition. Haled into court, Tintoretto was required to explain. It symbolized something; this much the judges thought they knew. Tintoretto disabused them. He said he put the dog there more or less by instinct, meaning genius. He might have added that merely symbolic art—art requiring a key—is always a door to a closet, whereas great art is an open door to great experience.

True it is that dogs have been employed to symbolize death, revenge, wisdom, loyalty and many other things besides. Yet all such tags are fleas to Tintoretto's modest and mysterious hound. This is a real dog and no mere symbol. It is a friend to man, not indifferent yet apart, self-sufficient, somehow. It has a cleanly and a staying look; it washes its own feet, one is sure. Its animal calm counterpoints the arduous brotherhood of the rest.

The Prado has another dog, very different and yet also immortal. Goya, grim prophet of a spiritually sterile age, created it. The suck of a shadowy abyss, and at its base a mutt's head lifted in imploring profile: that is the whole picture. What can it mean? One wants to rescue the dog first and ask questions later. But the dog is in another world, looking up and away to an invisible master. Heartless master, to abandon a little dog so! One yearns to hurl him into the abyss after his pet.

There is no master to condemn—unless it be Goya himself. He it was, after all, who doomed this dog. But then it is only a painted dog. Why on earth should one feel so strongly, personally, for something in a picture?

Goya put himself in the dog's place. He painted the dog with such passionate personal desperation and such mastery that everyone who sees the picture shares the desperation in some degree, and feels himself also to be the dog. Is Goya inveighing against cruelty to dogs, or against indifference to the death of animals? No, but against more. Consider the cruel indifference of the heavens, that see all living creatures on this earth go down to death. The dog looks imploringly to the heavens: its master is nowhere about. Still the picture is not only a protest. No masterpiece ever was that alone.

The dog is dying, drowning, absolutely. What is it to do? This is the rock-bottom question. The main reason why

Goya painted the picture was finally to suggest this question, and its answer as well. What is the answer? To implore no longer; to let go; to die free at least. In short, to cease to be a dog and become a man again, a free spirit even though drowning in the abyss.

Things-in-themselves, of course, were Goya's main concern. He was not a realist exactly—his art is all too black, too painfully self-contained for that. Rather, he was a realizer: a man determined to give things their full weight; though he found them heavy as a dinner of stones. This may seem no spiritual work, but it is. Every time the spirit sinks below the surface of history to run underground for a space, genius of Goya's kind appears and helps men, stranded as they are, make soundings. It is a way of finding strength in contact with hidden reality, whether painful or not.

The genius in a sterile age digs down to underground rivers and naturally finds them dark. Yet they quench his thirst and that of his fellows. He draws life from the dark streams. He crawls on his belly; he digs, scoops, slobbers a little—and rises refreshed, strong as a god. Thus Antaeus, the giant son of Mother Earth, sprang up revived from every fall. Goya may have thought of Antaeus the day he first pictured a huge, bowed, deep-backed, swarthy man seated on a mountain range, gazing dumbly over one shoulder at the stars. Or he may have had himself in mind.

Across the gallery from the drowning mutt sits another animal of Goya's: a black goat—as noble and solemn as a midnight Dionysius—enthroned in profile. He looks more human than anybody in the crescent of monstrous witches convened to do him homage. Or rather he looks less human. The witches' human qualities, one discovers, are just what horrify most. Goat-worship would be cleansing for such creatures; it could only do them good. Studying the witches as if with the goat's mild eye, one comes at last upon one's own face—more horrible than all the rest.

No human being is so pure that he cannot learn purity from a goat, nor too wise to gain wisdom at a witches' sabbath. The cup of wisdom is excess.

Picasso is plainly Goya's heir. Among his pictures of animals an early one, the Museum of Modern Art's *Boy Leading a Horse,* sets the stage. The boy is young Picasso; the resemblance is exact. The splendid misty horse is imagination. It does not symbolize imagination; it is imagination. In other words, this horse gives a clearer image of imagination than one has oneself. It does not represent, it embodies that most human and glorious of powers. The hooves trail into air. Bridle there is none. By an invisible halter, the boy is leading imagination into the desert of the twentieth century. Horrors lie ahead.

They burst out with *Guernica.* Historically this huge and shatteringly ugly picture is a shout of protest against the bombing of a defenseless Spanish town. It is also a return to Altamira, a dream-return, and a confession, made in agony for everyone, that the beasts are raging still untamed, destructively as cancer, through the soul of man. How has man advanced? Is history only an elaborate, murderous, interminable confidence game? Not likely, but this picture makes a person wonder.

Picasso paints by electric light. He prefers it, as being steadier. It may distort the colors but it keeps a single grip on the forms, instead of juggling them as firelight does, or slowly, smoothly revolving its grip as daylight does. Naturally, artificial light pervades Picasso's art: its use carries over into the subjective. *Guernica,* for instance, is a midnight scene, out of doors, seemingly composed of broken plaster and crumpled newspapers in the wind, lit by a kerosene lamp, a naked electric bulb suspended from nowhere, and also, one assumes, by an enormous flash, as of an exploding bomb, coming from in front of the picture. It is as if one's own head had exploded.

—Had exploded to destroy everything but its own images. Where Altamira showed reality welling up through the mind, *Guernica* shows mind obliterating reality. These images are projected flat against an infinite and always dangerous darkness. Driving through Kansas in the night at ninety miles an hour, swerving to avoid a snake and catching for that single instant in the glare of one's headlights a billboard advertising cigarettes, huge amidst nothingness, would be similar to seeing *Guernica*. On across Kansas, one fumbles for a cigarette. On across the gallery one fumbles, less hopefully, for Picasso's meaning.

After the impact of the whole, the details come as lesser and yet powerful shocks. That woman's breasts are thorning into each other. That man's fingers, curled about the broken, anachronistic sword, are nerveless and fat as sausages. That horse's torment spikes rustily, suffocatingly, up from his broken bowels through his mouth. Man's noblest conquest is the horse, yet an ignoble victim. The bull stands astonished by its own presence. Passing from madness to madness, it appears once in the night, and bellows once. Man's noblest victim is the bull, yet an ignoble conqueror. Itself numb with astonishment, the bull radiates hell to all the rest.

Since *Guernica* is admittedly hellish, why on earth did Picasso want to paint it? People keep asking this question and therefore it ought to be answered, along with a second question that usually follows the first: "Isn't he laughing up his sleeve?" Picasso may get a laugh at the people who pay ruinous prices for his every daub. His serious work, though, is dead-serious. Beauty has nothing to do with the case; emotional significance has everything. "They say that I can draw like Raphael," Picasso once complained. "All right, then why don't they leave me alone?" His ugly pictures cost him more effort than his lovely ones: they come out of suffering.

The purpose of tragedy is to indicate the eternal background of mortal striving. The good life shines against the dark of death: it has death to deny. Taken out of this context, virtue would become a mere game, a question of manners. Now, art shines against the dark of futility: it has hopelessness to fight. As one of the great tragic artists, Picasso keeps pointing to this.

A minor sculpture of Picasso's, a pregnant ape, elucidates his nightmare side. The ape looks like a cross between a fertility idol and a guardian demon. In bronze its belly seems as heavy as a cannon ball, and painfully taut besides. Its tautness leads one to imagine that the belly in the model from which the cast was made must have been a child's beach-ball. There obviously was a toy car for the head, with grinning bumper-snout and windshield eyes. This might be the work of a man who, abandoned by his family, solaces himself by playing with its relics. Below that level, the sculpture says that every man's creative energies are now sickeningly perverted.

Zeus gave birth to Athena from his head. Man, the intelligent ape, strains, grins, and makes a motor car. Indeed man's head, the palace of intelligence, has itself become a car, no longer a temple, and his thoughts mere tourists. Meanwhile, the new that is in humanity—a creation of heart and soul, of genitals and genes and not just mind—kicks and smothers in the sinking womb.

The *Man with a Lamb*, at Vallouris, is more ambitious and perhaps more hopeful. It stands in the village square:

a life-size, shadow-dappled bronze of a man wearily carrying a bound victim. This would not be the Good Shepherd: the beast is either to be marketed or sacrificed. Assume it will be marketed: then the sculpture is a Marxist monument with little mystery about it. Picasso claims to be a Marxist, so it may be that the animal stands for bodily nourishment and nothing more. In materialistic thinking, a man's whole work is to supply his fellows' bodily needs. The true hero is a material producer. The victim will be devoured; the man will have the thanks of his community. And how much more deserving he does seem, oblivious upon his pedestal, than the usual bronze brandishers of swords and thoughtful scratchers of the chest one usually finds in public parks!

This would make the *Man with a Lamb* a tasteful monument to a materialist idea, no more. But there is greatness in the sculpture, too. As so often happens, its greatness takes the form of a question. And as usual the superficial meaning of the piece is precisely what is called into question. "When I draw a straight line," Picasso once remarked in conversation, "it's a straight line. And when I draw a curve it's a curve." Then he smiled gently. The words and smile together expressed a certain tension between the obvious and the mysterious. This tension is half the life of great art, and of the *Man with a Lamb*.

The form heightens the tension: one can tell at a glance a good deal about what the statue represents, although a city man at least would be hard put to say whether the animal was really a lamb or perhaps a goat. The sculpture's details remain permanently cloudy. It is so roughly—artfully roughly—formed that one cannot be sure if the man is ugly or handsome, clothed or naked, solemn or joyful. The sculpture as a whole resembles, not other monuments, but ancient votive statuary. In its ancient models the goat would be a sacrifice to a god, and the man would be a supplicant hoping for a sign. Thus Picasso's models were just the opposite of materialistic, and they shape one's second thoughts about the statue. This bronze man bearing a bronze animal through sunshine, storm, shadow, starlight, winter, dawn and summer again around the years, what is he really? Is he worker, or seeker?

What is man? This question stands at the heart of Picasso's life-work. And the very question shows that man with his animals has come a little distance after all.

Chapter 10

Mirrors of Death and Life

REALITY IS FIRE, ONE VAST SACRIFICIAL FIRE, IN the leaf and in blood and in the stars, one fire. Here the Persians and the physicists agree.

Who shall picture the surface, the skin of fire?

To paint a literal copy of a tree would be to parody its tree-ness. True realism, therefore, is not literal but magical. It sets a chill mirror opposite the fire, in a darkened room.

One day Leonardo's father brought home a small round panel and suggested that the boy paint something on it. First Leonardo straightened and polished the panel, until it shone like a mirror. For the next few weeks he dodged about the fields, returning at evening with bats, lizards, snakes and butterflies in his hands. He was constructing in the privacy of his room a miniature monster out of their dismembered and re-assembled parts. The monsters of mythology are mostly combinations of known creatures.

When his little horror was complete, Leonardo probably

suspended it from strings in the dusky room. Then he copied it exactly on his panel, just as if he had caught it in a mirror. The multiple corpse was done away with. The room was darkened; one pale ray brushed Leonardo's finished panel. He invited his father in for a look—and scared the old man half to death. "The work," said Leonardo with a smile, "answers the purpose for which it was made."

Neither the physical light of the world nor its spiritual light can be gazed on directly. One sees through a glass darkly, by reflections, by seeing what the light illuminates. Yet no one ever saw the sun in the moon or his true self in a mirror. Narcissus was not such an ass to be so deceived, but he fell for the physical—and drowned.

Mirrors reflect the corpse that one carries. Their quality is quicksilver: swiftness in stillness. Certain monsters are not allowed to look in mirrors. Leonardo forced his to do so. The boy held a mirror up to fable and made it real, terrifying. That was his purpose. Now he would go on to hold an ever more perfect mirror up to ever loftier conceptions. His realism would become the polished shield of the philosopher. And the dart of his imagination would become a clouded thunderbolt.

A lovely girl is gazing into a dark mirror where she sees not her own face but a grinning death's head. This recurs often in popular Renaissance art. It is a moral anecdote, a *memento mori,* and a good deal more. Mirrors are magical. Frequently and solemnly invoked, they can age and uglify anyone. When they are worshiped they can even kill. This the skull confides, clackingly. And those who stare too long at the moon are courting the night when it will swoop and fly into their gaping mouths like a cold groan come back to float down their gullets and shatter the stained glass of their viscera. Madness, in short.

Caravaggio once painted in the mirror an insane self-portrait, as Medusa, with snakes for hair. He showed himself bitten to agony by the vipers of his own brain. This reflected flesh with its crown of snakes was also Caravaggio's enemy. In spirit he played the part of Perseus, who turned Medusa to stone by showing her own reflection to the monster in a polished shield. Perseus had petrified Medusa with fright at her own visage, and Caravaggio proposed to do the same with his nightmare self.

The early Greeks pictured Perseus' victory on their burial urns as a sign that death could be conquered. The story of David and Goliath has some of the same significance. Goliath's threats were like the boasts of death personified and seemingly invincible. Blake painted him therefore as a giant Death. Even more tellingly, Michelangelo left Goliath unshaped, and made his *David* naked and alone, with a look of searching, since death moves everywhere.

Twice Caravaggio painted David holding the head of Goliath. These canvases, at the Borghese Palace and in Vienna, make Goliath's head a death emblem comparable to Medusa's. Her head retained the power to petrify, and Perseus used it as a weapon. Caravaggio's *David* seems to do the same with the head of Goliath. Caravaggio makes David thrust Goliath's head forward right to the surface of the canvas. That ruined brow presses outwards urgently and horribly: one could almost poke a thumb in the hole. But young David himself stands outside of the picture, on the far side as it were, beyond the looking-glass. He might at any moment drop the head, or release it rather, leaving it stuck like a ham to glass on the inside surface of the picture, and go. Like oneself looking in a mirror, he is free to go.

It is a relief to come upon his less grand but peaceful pictures of Saint Jerome: one at the Borghese Palace and the other hidden away in the cloister at Montserrat. These bring back the death's head, in the conventional form of a skull on the saint's desk: it holds no terrors. One supposes that the saint keeps the skull not as a reminder of coming death, certainly not as something to face down, but rather to recall that art is long and life is short, that he has work to do, that dust is dust in the service of God, and finally that these bones will rise again. It is a companionable skull, far more friendly than a mirror would be.

Of all those who followed Leonardo's and Caravaggio's lead into the quicksilver country of mirror-realism, Velásquez was the one who stayed to rule. Like those ancients cursed of earth, who could find peace only upon islands formed by rivers, Velásquez built his palace on the strand between reality and illusion.

He has been called "baroque" but in fact Velásquez' humanism culminates the Renaissance. He was not mannered though he mirrored a mannered age. He was not stylish but solid, not grandiloquent but simply mighty.

Velásquez was a kind of Theseus, whose Minotaur lay not in the labyrinth but in mirrors. He rid his mirror-world of monsters, and proved it possible to mirror life as well as death.

Theseus, to settle a border dispute, once raised a column inscribed: *This is not the Peloponnesus, but Ionia!* And on the reverse: *This is not Ionia, but the Peloponnesus!* A similar column guards the thresholds of Velásquez' pictures, inscribed on the outside: *This is not reality, but illusion!* And on the *inside: This is not illusion, but reality!*

The very air before Velásquez' *Weavers,* at the Prado, seems to tremble and hum. The subject, taken from Ovid, is the weaving contest between divine Athena and a Greek girl named Arachne. Arachne won, but Athena then transformed her into a spider. The truth is that the Spider-Mother, who spins out of her belly, is an older goddess than Athena. She is fate that spins. So Arachne's metamorphosis could not have been more honorable. It meant that she had taken the workings of fate into herself. Arachne was a mother of free will.

Whether life is a shroud or a cocoon, every mother's son must weave his own. He weaves the spider-thread of his own free will, a gossamer that binds up his past, present and future. Remembering and hoping, he chooses for the future. Only such time-conscious choosing is free. Man spins free will out of experience, in hope. Hence the qualities of memory, immediacy and inviting mystery in Velásquez' *Weavers.* All three together are appropriate to the theme.

Led irresistibly within the picture one stands amazed as at a turning point in life. While art, illusion and reality are meshing behind one they open out ahead into what is woven: Athena's fateful tapestry and brave Arachne's—luminous, impalpable and real as tomorrow.

Hermes' victories are never complete, but Velásquez rejoiced in them. *Hermes and Argus* is among his greatest canvases. Argus was the Night Sky, who guarded the Moon Cow, Io, with all his thousand eyes. Hermes was the god of merchants, thieves, travelers and scientists. His metal, mercury, made mirrors, medicines and alchemical gold.

Hermes played sleepy tunes to Argus until every one of all those thousand eyes had closed. Then he killed him and freed Io.

Thus daylight consciousness prevailed over darkling primitive thought. Trade, thievery, travel, philosophy and science partly supplanted outright robbery and superstition. To celebrate all this, Velásquez, the humanist, painted two splendid men. One of them is dozing off. The other peers at him and seems about to rise, sword in hand. There is a soft, massive, cloudlike eagerness about the waiting cow, like a ghost at midnight.

Velásquez' *Venus* at the National Gallery in London is as saucily incarnate as a movie star. A slim young lady lying on a bed with her back turned smiles into a hand-mirror. Her mirror is like a small reflection of the looking-glass through which one has stepped to assault her.

One can see her face in the mirror—complacent, smiling and a little plain. She is looking at oneself, in her mirror.

Velásquez' most celebrated canvas, *The Serving Maids* at the Prado, was done directly from a huge mirror. Oneself is the mirror, in fact, from which one could bend to touch the sleepy dog in the foreground—if a mirror could reach out. Being put in the position of the mirror, flattened into place, gives one a feeling of subjective unreality and immobility as opposed to the objective life in the picture. It is odd, but one feels dead, somehow. In his passion to show aliveness within his art, Velásquez hints at death outside of it. He mirrors the arrow at one point in its course. Is it falling, or flying? Which are we? Velásquez brings the quality of doubt together with monumentality.

Calm, trivial, huge, true and very strange is *The Serving Maids.*

A little page boy seems to be kicking the dog, which pays no attention. After a time one sees that the page is merely resting his foot on the dog's back and trying to balance meanwhile, hands outstretched, in obedience to Velásquez' wish that nobody move. Nearby stands a dwarf maid who seems halfway convinced, through Velásquez' interest, of her own great dignity. At the center of it all the little Infanta gazes without interest into the mirror. She is lovely, pinchable, and seems in doubt of everything, even of her elegant, comfortless clothes. This unhappy princess of the blood, on whom great alliances depend, fragile as a flower and as rooted fast, is attended by two lovely ladies who cannot help her.

Velásquez himself is also in the picture, stepping from before his canvas, his brush held lightly and firmly as a fencer's foil, his eyes dark, heavy, searching. Far behind him a mirror dimly reflects the King and Queen—or any visitor and his wife—in little. For a while, as intended, this fanciful reflection makes one forget the real mirror represented by the picture surface.

There is a staircase at the very back, with a shadowy bearded figure ascending or descending to or from a dream. Staircases are unresting.

The Serving Maids seems almost as much a memory as it is a mirror-image. Yet mirrors are notoriously forgetful, and one's memories can never be so slickly solid and complete as what the mirror shows. The eye of imagination sees more sparkle and less matter than does the looking-glass. The glass stares steadily, squarely, while mental vision darts and twists and soars like a live thing.

The picture both reflects and promises something impossible: a solid exactitude of mind-sight. The illusion of it is so gripping that if somebody happens to step between oneself and the canvas, that person appears as a mere wraith.

In the flesh one is submerged, so to speak, and sees what one must see. Imaginative vision is only partly submerged, like the elves and sprites of legend. It is fickle Ariel, fraught with natural magics. Also it is a man's first frail hope of surpassing himself. Half the disciplines of the mystics are designed to give imaginative vision more direction. Half the disciplines of art are designed to give it more vividness. When these two disciplines are combined in one man, his imagination soars like Velásquez'.

In dreams and mirrors, one tends to see oneself as mature when one is young and youthful when one is old. One seems to be gliding above the years in a distant and nostalgic mood—whether distant from the past or nostalgic for the future. Something similar happens in looking at Velásquez' pictures. *The Serving Maids* is a release from the enclosing world, a dream to be awakened into.

Rapt in Velásquez' reality—dreaming, mirroring and already remembering only that—one is like a three-year-old child sitting unnoticed at the head of the stairs. The grownups are having a party by candlelight down below.

Three-years-old is not yet submerged. The child looks down from a cloud of glory, bearing witness and admiring with all his heart. Gods, the grownups seem to him.

How could they ever guess that the child is right, these ignorant laughing human gods, except through Velásquez? —Whose imaginative vision soared to three-years-old at the top of the stairs.

Chapter 11

Truth in Beauty

EVERYBODY POURS OUT LOVE NOW AND THEN INTO something he sees. It may be a girl with long bronze hair or a mountain green with pines, or just a housefly scrubbing its iridescent eyes. In any case he pours himself out towards it as if thinking: "You and I are one!"

Such passionate identification is just what the great artist keeps demonstrating. Love takes him to his own limits and beyond. Surely this visual sort of love is the opposite of blind. The question is, what causes it?

A thing, or an idea, or both together?

Beauty, or truth, or both together?

To philosophers, ideas are in themselves the very breath of life. Hence the philosophic view that art must serve ideas—especially the idea of beauty. One might almost think of beauty as a single perfection—invisible, eternal, unattainable—and of art as a sacrifice upon her altar. But this implies a hierarchy of art, with relative perfection at the top, and grotesqueries at the bottom. Perhaps the

Greeks would not have seen the difficulty here, since they believed that every art except their own must be bad. In sculpture they would doubtless have elected Phidias chief. But if he came closest then Michelangelo distorted the ideal, the Chinese and Indians missed it altogether, and the Africans were carving outer darkness.

Not even from the Acropolis can one see around the world.

Philosophers keep casting intellectual nets into the sea of existence. A few of them believe that artists do something similar on a cruder level, casting visual nets into the sea of nature. Artists, they maintain, describe nature in order to edify mankind, and embellish it in order to give pleasure. This amounts to placing the artist halfway between scientists and decorators. Seurat, whose careful decorations were built on his own theory of optics, might have accepted the position. "They see poetry in what I have done," he once complained. "No, I apply my method and that is all there is to it." Yet the sad, persistent whisper of poetry in Seurat's art belies him.

A more formidable example of the artist who stands between the scientist and the decorator would be Leonardo: he includes all three. Leonardo gave as much time to science as to art, and he made his living mostly by designing Sforza's pageants and grand balls. His notes on painting are proto-scientific; he kept preaching the exact imitation of nature. Yet what Leonardo himself practiced was not imitation but identification with nature.

The difference is vast. Leonardo's most earnestly descriptive drawings of plants, rocks and water do not describe so much as caress, nor show so much as celebrate what he saw. The beauty of these drawings springs neither from nature alone nor from the artist alone, but from both together, like lovers. Leonardo's style, therefore, is not a matter of personal idiosyncrasy like handwriting. Such a master's style is formed in loving struggle with nature. It outlines both his own limitations and the splendors of the world beyond.

Every great work of art creates a new center, from which a new kind of vision radiates. To artists, visions—not ideas—are the breath of life. Nor can visions aspire to beauty. Either they have it or they don't.

How can philosophy—how can anything—bind the muse of art? She lives in visions: flashing, contradictory, myriad, always personal and ever new.

Modern art abandons beauty in the commonest sense of the word—which is prettiness—precisely because that sort of beauty gives general delight. It has ceased to have personal value by becoming public property. Many a pretty girl who must daily smart under the slyly possessive glances of strangers knows about this. She never asked to be the world's ice cream; she wants to mean something to someone. Artists are the same. Yet one could no more eliminate true beauty from art than women from the world.

Mirror, mirror on the wall,
Who is the fairest one of all?

Most girls and boys grow up to be witches and ogres in some degree. Prototypes in fairy tales can teach a lot to any mother or father who muses humbly upon them while the children dream.

In *The House Above the Trees* a beautiful wicked witch threatens a little girl, who asks the forest what to do. Rustling quietly the forest says, "Ignore her." From the days of Delilah and old Troy until last Saturday night, men have been trying to distinguish true beauty from false. Were there some way to make this distinction with assurance, then love and loneliness would partition between them the continent of romance—that perpetual New World.

Of the methods that men do possess, the forest one is the best. False beauty bends its rays upon itself. So the forest ignores it, in a sense, by remaining dark. True beauty on the other hand illuminates the darkest wood, like candles in a cathedral.

Look away from beauty to see how it shines.

Beauty appears to be one aspect of everything. This accounts for its infinite variety and contradictory ways, yet it makes beauty no easier to recognize. What are its distinguishing qualities? Three, say philosophers: "Wholeness, harmony, and radiance." Raphael's *Saint George and the Dragon,* at the National Gallery in Washington, has all three of these. Are they sufficient? Raphael knew how to shift his focus from whole acres to a single blade of grass. No precision of line or abundance of detail could tear so flexible an imagination as his. To create a sense of self-containment—wholeness—he surveyed Saint George's struggle as if through the wrong end of a telescope. The very smallness of the panel, less than a foot high, enhances that first quality.

Being removed some distance from one's own more fragmentary struggles also lends harmony to the scene, and this second quality is assisted by the limpid light and the breezy courtship of contours throughout the picture. Finally the picture's inner radiance, eliminating shadows and all ugliness, offers basketfuls of small, glowing delights as simply as if they were wild strawberries. Yet all this wholeness, harmony and radiance together cannot make *Saint George* a masterpiece. Why not?

Masterpieces must have something more besides; call it

significance. For, unlike Raphael's masterpieces this particular panel is only a chivalric pleasantry: soothing, delightful, pointless. But perhaps significance comes under the philosophers' third heading: radiance. Beauty shines not only to the eye but also to the mind. It is one aspect of all things—including thought.

Beauty can be as clear as a doorbell. Therefore it is a source not only of visual joy but of intellectual joy as well. This joy is not to be equated with mere pleasure; it is more like an awakening.

To speak of beauty as a source of pleasure, merely, would be like describing love as a source of advantage. Love is advantageous, as beauty is pleasurable, and both are human satisfactions, but only a cold glutton would describe them so. Beauty like love is an awakening, fructifying thing: they both contain the seeds of something beyond.

The subject matter of most masterpieces was commissioned by a patron—true. Nobody pretends that paints in the tube and in a masterpiece are the same. Why should there be any greater degree of identity between the ideas in a patron and the ideas in the masterpiece that he commissioned? Subject matter has often been assigned to the artist and sometimes a symbolic significance alien to him has been imposed on his work. He is not necessarily responsible for these. Yet the living significance, the seed of intellectual joy in a masterpiece, has got to come from the artist himself.

Technical competence and the ability to follow instructions never made a master, nor even a whole man, for that matter. It is not skill, let alone slavishness, that distinguishes the masterpiece, but rather an illuminating force, a radiant seed of truth.

If every masterpiece is so by nature of its seed-truth, why are not these seeds of truth recognized and agreed upon? The answer is that they flower mainly in the heart, each time different. Still, the seed-truth in a masterpiece does keep making itself known. They call Bruegel "the Peasant Painter." Few people recognize the fact that Bruegel had a mind at all, much less that he was one of the profoundest thinkers in history. And yet because he goes on speaking to the heart, he lives.

The ancient worshiper in the Parthenon did not need to be told that he moved within a work designed for the illumination of his soul. He knew that. Is the tourist wiser?

But why should Bruegel's light flower so darkly, felt and yet unrecognized? One reason is simply that, like the Parthenon, Bruegel is physically far to seek. Almost all his best work is at Vienna. Another reason is that copies of Bruegel painted by his son—and often misleadingly labeled plain "Bruegel"—are scattered everywhere. These copies are exceedingly expert, but dead; they are dead husks of seeds. In fact the son had a way of omitting from his copies only the most significant details, probably because they disturbed him. Bruegel had admitted the boy to the mysteries of his craft, but not of his thought. This is by the way, however. Even the most faithful copy is painted with the hand and eye alone instead of with a man's whole being, and must therefore be dead. A copy is an automaton.

The third reason for Bruegel's relative obscurity is that very little has been written about him. Literary criticism outstrips that of art. For every word on Bruegel there are a thousand on Shakespeare, mostly concerning his inner meanings. Those on Bruegel deal mostly with style, origins and influences—academic questions. As for Bruegel's purpose in painting, it is assumed that he just wanted to give pleasure, for a fee. He did want to be enjoyed, of course, but only to prepare the ground. Shakespeare entertained for the same purpose, to prepare the ground. Once the ground is ready and prepared these twin geniuses come walking, high as clouds, sowing the seeds of truth.

Seed-truths can resemble dragon-seeds at times, which may be one reason why Bruegel sowed his so deep. One's first impression of his *Crucifixion* is a vast wet brown landscape of early spring, alive with festival. After a time one sees deep in the center Jesus fallen under his cross. But the top part of the cross is blocked from view, so that it resembles instead the humble, T-shaped "cross of man"—of the not-yet-saved. Calvary, in the distance, appears to be crowned with yet another instrument of torture, death and return: the cartwheel atop a tall pole.

On another hill, fantastically eroded, stands that most forlorn of buildings, a broken windmill. This weird hill with its broken mill is perhaps all that remains of the ancient Tower of Babel. Spring, with its warm rains and the blood of Christ, is bringing a new world into this ancient one. Everywhere is the circling of the new, a dance of life, filled with health, horror and hope.

A third hill rises at the very base of the scene, and this is where the Marys are grieving, in a semicircle, with their backs to the rest of picture. They seem oddly conventional figures for Bruegel to have painted, as if he had removed himself from them instead of participating to the full as usual. Frozen with sorrow, the women are gazing up and out of the picture, toward oneself.

What can they be doing down there? They cluster at the foot of the True Cross, where, invisible, crucified, are you.

No, it is true. Only look up and see the ravens circling

close. Gaze all around—for there is time, and no agony yet —if you would witness the human condition through more-than-human eyes.

One's eyes are a dark, sparkling medium between two lights: the light of the world and that of the mind. But the invisible eye of imagination is itself contained in darkness: the darkness of one's own infinity. In a sense it is the fitfully sparkling, slowly mounting sun of that infinity, lighting the invisible in the vast. It was Bruegel's task to strengthen this invisible eye in man, this poor, dark, sparkling, painfully rising sun, this coal of God. And the means that Bruegel chose, in a world that has never yet known him or comprehended what he brought, was to offer again and again the invisible within oneself.

Like so many Bruegels, *The Wedding Feast* gives delight to social historians. They love explaining that the feast takes place in a barn because the father of the bride would not have had sufficient room in his farmhouse. That much clarified, they dodge around the table identifying relatives and guests such as the priest, the familiar tosspot and the condescending squire with his hound. How quaint, they say, to hang a rich cloth over the stacked hay in back of the bride! How quaint—and how observant Bruegel must have been to notice—that the pies are carried in upon a door! And so forth. In fact the rich cloth half-covering the hay, and the pies upon the door, both show how temporal are human feasts. As usual with Bruegel, such details are not only accurate but significant. To see them as a quaint sort of documentation is not to see them.

Who or where is the bridegroom at *The Wedding Feast*? Here the social historians either quarrel or fall silent. In studying pictures one should never try to answer such a question outright. The impatient search goes in circles. It is better to follow one's eyes, in a spirit of trust. In the present case that means following the pies—dark ones for the guests and white for the bride and groom—not only because they look so delicious but also because they have just been carried under one's own nose, past one's position in the naked doorway just outside the picture. One sees the pies, and then the wine, clear wine. One is hungry, and a-thirst. Good! Here understanding also starts.

It appears that the last of the wine is being poured. There are lots of empty pots. Can this be the wedding at Cana? Possibly, for Christ moves throughout Bruegel's art. Yet one imagines that the bride at Cana must have been beautiful, whereas this one seems downright homely at first. She looks heavy, stupid and smug in her abundance.

Yet the whole *Wedding Feast* is filled to brimming with beauty, which radiates from the plain-seeming bride. When one looks back to her, the bride begins to change. She glows and changes like the harvest moon, so that what seemed to be complacency at first becomes all pleasure now, and what seemed smugness turns into devotion, into such love as would revive a dying man and make him reach out for her blessing.

Who was the groom at Cana? Ah, fellow husbands, who but ourselves?

And the water changed to wine? Mankind is matter, sensation and idea. These things interpenetrate in art as well, and beauty embraces them together.

Chapter 12

How to Just Imagine

IMAGINATION IS THE SPECIFICALLY HUMAN FORCE. Blushing and worshiping both pre-suppose it. They show imagination at its perigee and apogee—like Mutt and Jeff.

Dreaming, divining and even driving a car require imagination. At a hundred and fifty miles an hour a great racing driver may appear to be doing nothing at all. But he has made himself a part of the car and is therefore feeling, and in a sense doing, everything the car does. To imagine really well is also to make oneself the quiet and seemingly inactive part of something terribly powerful and fast. At the same time it requires a firm grip on lasting truths. To race along a highway is possible only because the highway itself does not move. Likewise to race along a path of air is possible only so long as the path remains firm.

A rainbow dragon materializes. It can go anywhere in a moment. The hard thing is to make it go slow and keep to the wide wandering paths aloft. To be free, and free of illusion.

Leonardo recommended to young artists a device that he had found "extremely useful in arousing the mind to various inventions. When you look at a stained wall, or one built of mingled stones, you may find a resemblance to landscapes, with mountains, rivers, rocks, trees, wide valleys and hills in varied arrangement; or you may see battles and men in action or strange faces and costumes—an endless variety."

Children are best at this kind of seeing. A three-year-old at breakfast can look at an orange peel on the table, see it plain as day, and at the same time envision, in and through the orange peel, a ship on the wide ocean. Or at supper with the grownups in the garden, he may actually see the bread crumbs and the Roquefort on the dark polished table as reflections of the stars and moon. Such miracles are commonplace: adults hardly notice.

Children's schools, as they are now set up, lead the eye of imagination inward from the physical world. Bent upon a book, it learns to form visions out of words. Who has not seen Shylock, or Anna Karenina pulling on her gloves of a snowy evening, or Gatsby in white flannels, or terrific Moby Dick, or Long John Silver smoking in his narrow galley, or Mark Twain's whole meandering Mississippi tilted into print?

The boy blissfully reading *Huckleberry Finn,* the youth weeping over Tolstoy, and once in a great while a museum visitor, are all exalted with imaginative vision. Nobody can keep it up for long, however; it is not only strenuous in itself but also wildly susceptible to distraction. Often it becomes the prey of sloth, dying of disuse over the years.

Suicide of the imaginative vision is as crippling as it is popular. The totally unimaginative man may seem all right; he may even perform intellectual tasks of a difficult sort; he may be as stuffed with facts as an encyclopedia, and yet he cannot think: he merely learns, and repeats without improvement.

Intellection without a substratum of imagination is like fist-fighting without footwork. What distinguishes the boxer from the mere brawler is footwork and what distinguishes the thinker from the mere intellectual is imagination. And yet to "be imaginative" is nothing in itself. Imagination is not a state, but a way.

The man in Dostoevski's *The Possessed* who suggested solving the problem of poverty by slaughtering the poor was a serious thinker with one serious lack: imagination. So is the man who seriously asks the question whether, to save one's own children from destruction, one would press a button killing all the children of another land. Only someone who had died to imagination could press that button. And once he had pressed it, imagination would return upon him in the shape of bat-winged, relentless Furies.

Except when dreaming or reading, the adult generally squints his eye of imagination. He seems to think in words, not images. More often, it may be, the images created in his mind are blotted out by what he is actually seeing.

Behind closed eyes, pictures instantly form. They are the natural dress of thought. Even the mathematician formulating a theorem "sees" the numbers and symbols falling into place. Newton "saw" gravity in an apple's fall. Goethe said he had the power to see in and through an actual blossom its entire cycle of growth and decay, all in a moment.

In childhood the eye of imagination served fantasy—that airy bridge to insight. With the awakening of genius it comes to serve insight directly. The creative genius has gained his freedom without ceasing to be objective.

The child saw the ship through the orange peel. Was not the one as real as the other? The architect may find in that same orange peel a roof-section. The physicist may find a path of energy. The philosopher may find an image of the human condition. The painter may find a glowing fragment of the sun itself, ready for thrusting deep into the cool glade of his canvas. Of all such happy discoveries, imaginative vision is the source.

A more usual kind of discovery is the lucky hit made in the course of academic or scientific research. In every few shiploads of oysters, a pearl must lurk. The historian poring over musty Latin manuscripts may find a lost perversion of Tiberius. While infecting mice with strange diseases, the biochemist may chance upon a cure for baldness. Such achievements can be interesting and sometimes extremely beneficial in themselves, yet sages and artists have no wish to make them. The creatively wise man sits beneath a different tree—not the tree of knowledge but the tree of life. Instead of prying for pearls, he creates them. Instead of seeking gold he makes it at home. He is a treasury without a lock. Riches materialize upon his glance.

Were the wise also competitive, they might change the world. But this is to suggest an impossibility. *The strong man guardeth his house,* and the wise man's house is peace.

Adults generally settle for words in place of images, but children know instinctively that words by themselves are inadequate. Therefore children turn to drawing as a natural thing. Doodles—that vast sprawling underground of art—show the drawing instinct submerged in the adult, and yet not entirely submerged. Everyone would like to improve his doodles—to make the chimney straighter, the smoky spiral more relaxed and the cow less like a dog.

Cows are sure of themselves; they have an aura of inevitability—as if there were a primal cow for them to resemble. The same goes for tulips, robins, Christmas trees and the round-eyed bear. Some kinds of people, too, seem archetypal, such as pirates, princesses, witches and locomotive engineers. All these are basic images. So are certain abstract shapes: blocks, marbles, ice-cream cones, jackstraws, dewdrops, and dominoes. Again with colors, one should know them all—from fire-engine red to subtle salmon, emerald, saffron, yellow roses, bruises, apricots, bronze-colored hair and morning glories, and so on.

Far more than words or numbers are such images the raw material of creative thought. So it should be part of education to learn to picture them at will—passably in actual drawing and painting, and splendidly in the mind.

To plunge within a masterpiece is marvelous training for the eye of imagination. To make a serious and reverent effort oneself to draw and paint is fine, too. But certain inner disciplines can also help. The simplest of these is to close one's eyes, relax, and see what images may come. This means abandoning intellectual control, refusing all verbal intrusions of the mind, deliberately suspending thought. One is like a spectator passive and alone in the dark of a movie house, watching the screen.

In perfect calm will wild things unfold. Those sparkling zigzags that drift within one's closed eyelids may shortly settle down to be park-railings, and then turn into crocodiles with rusty teeth; their tails dissolving like sunset clouds as they sink below the glassy ocean—only to reappear, entwined in miniature: a polished cleat upon the sailboat deck.

It is all one and all changing. Coppery crocodiles turning to polished brass. The sea sulfurous. The sail as purple as a cloud. A skull and crossbones flaps at the masthead. How brave the pirates must have been, to sail under such a flag! But now thought intrudes. And the intensity of colors under one's eyelids shows that it must be getting light outside. Time for breakfast.

In sleep the eye of imagination awakened. Dreams were man's first awesome proof that he is spirit as well as flesh. If dogs dream too, they have similar proof, though what they make of it dog only knows. Who can deny that in dreams a man escapes the body? Any dull fellow will display in dreams a force and freedom of imagination rivaling Rabelais or Picasso. In every man, therefore, the eye of imagination is just as real as the physical eyes.

Dreams are precise but uncontrollable and fabulously swift. The light-keeper's wife is dreaming of her cat, which puts on boots and tells the time while fleetingly its blunt cat-face assumes the pointed features of a mouse. The single squeak of a real mouse has encompassed her entire dream. In dreams as in the flesh, seeing is believing. Were this true of the mind's eye in waking life as well, one would be insane.

A line of white sea birds, flying low, crosses the blue water of a bay. There is a mirror in a lighthouse bedroom, where the sea birds also fly for a moment. The light-keeper's wife has seen them in the mirror. Now, closing her eyes, she tries to call them back. What species were they? She forgot to notice. How many? She does not know. Well then, what does the eye of her imagination perceive?

White asterisks in the shadow of a cloud. Notes of music breaking into sunshine. The paper-trail of a kidnaped elf. Snowflakes on a string. Sea birds!

Simply to remember is also to imagine, to re-create. Therefore another step in tempering the imagination is to plunge it into the cold seas of memory, recalling to the dark of one's mind the people and places that one loved best of all—swimming through a deep succession of their images, separate in time and space.

Nothing except art itself so strengthens, stretches and heightens one's imaginative vision. The exercise could not be healthier, though it is hard at first, and bitter besides. Sometimes in the practice of imaginative vision, enemies, nightmare experiences, most embarrassing moments and ranklings of old wrongs will spring into consciousness, blocking the view. These ought to be ignored. To forgive but not forget is hell. To forget but not forgive is much better.

In learning to look, imagination must also learn to look away. Without this double discipline comes danger. A person with a persecution mania, for example, has developed only one side of his imagining power and will suffer acutely. So will cowards, and the jealous. Beyond that, nobody is strong enough to keep on facing down the many hateful visions that imagination keeps conjuring up. Just as in the body one takes care to avoid collisions, infections and similar dangers, so in the imagination also one must turn away from certain things, by a movement of the imagination itself.

The guardian demons at the thresholds of oriental temples and the gargoyles peering down from cathedral roofs are meant as warnings against casual entry, for things of the spirit are dangerous as well as good. The same is true of imaginative vision.

Sometimes imagination comes as a cloudburst. One can no more control it than bestride a cloud. Uncontrolled and ephemeral are one's re-creative powers! One drops into mere daydreams, regrets, recriminations, black remorse. The past swings and crashes like ocean breakers. It is gone, all gone, and how little one has been aware! The waste of life!

Yet after much practice the waters of the years fall still and begin to clear a little. Soaring high above them, one sees one's own shadow glide the ocean floor, miles down. One is flying over the past, at liberty, the sun on one's shoulders.

In Bruegel's *Icarus* a setting sun dominates all else. One gazes straight across the airy distances to its throne at the center. Air carries the colors of the sun, and also an approaching storm. Tiny galleons are fleeing for shelter. The sea curves transparently away. There is a man fishing from the cliff. Below him, plunging into the sea, is a momentary flash of legs—Icarus. He must have been falling since noontime, when the sun was high. Icarus flew too high towards the sun, which melted the wax of his wings. Now he and the sun are going down together. Icarus will never return.

Is this picture a pure puff of magic: idle, ephemeral and innocent of all philosophy? The same thing might be said of *The Tempest,* and as soon denied. *Icarus* has the same wild yet crystalline mood as *The Tempest.* Each holds in precarious suspension the same classic elements: air, water, earth, and fire. Shakespeare and Bruegel used to balance the very elements like a cloud of butterflies upon their fingertips.

On the crest of the headland a man is plowing, folding back the earth as neatly as a counterpane. Someone sleeps in the bushes nearby. A shepherd stands gazing up into the sky—whether astonished by the fall of Icarus or troubled by the approaching storm. Where can the father be? Where is Daedalus? He warned his boy against flying too high or too low. Daedalus himself soared along the middle course, borne on transparent air.

Icarus fell. Daedalus, lamenting, flew on and vanished into the sunset.

Bruegel was, like Daedalus, a mighty artificer. He may well have warned his own boy of the dangers in imaginative life. When imagination flies too high towards the terrible fire of the spirit, or too low towards the stormy waters of sense, disaster threatens.

Yet, all in all, Bruegel's *Icarus* is even more of an invitation than it is a warning. Earth, air and water bring life and afterwards death, for they are of the turning world. But the life of this world itself is fire, terrible and heavenly, poured from without. Inside Bruegel's picture men are gazing upon earth, air and water. From outside, one stares straight through to fire, to the sun. One's vision soars into the sunset. One becomes Daedalus, and shares in his experience.

Finally the green shadow of one's imagining self dwindles away to nothing as the ocean floor descends and vanishes. Now there is no land anywhere, no memories. And the sun is setting. Yet imagination strongly wings on into the sun.

One creates! Purely one creates! Ah, this is no reshaping; this is the unknown, the new, the coming into life!

Chapter 13

Painters, Saints and Savages

THE BEAUTIES OF NATURE ARE ALL OF A PIECE, flowing and wheeling together. The dusk that follows the sunset and the stars that come out one by one overhead all seem part of a single process, a single significance. Nature everywhere appears to reflect God's will. Not so with art. A masterpiece reflects the free will of the man who made it. Having its center in itself, it stands apart from all the rest of creation. So a masterpiece can be understood only as one person understands another; by sympathetic intuition.

It is not enough to admire or to loathe a fellow-man: one tries to put oneself in his place. The same with art: One tries to abandon one's own center in order to center one's perceptions within the masterpiece itself. This means imaginative exploration and much more besides.

It requires among other things a kind of reverence, a still gratitude, but definitely not admiration. The moment one stops to say, "Isn't that lovely!" one is in danger of losing the way. More, one has the experience of being transported as by magic some distance off the path of beauty—it may be a foot or a mile. To be caught up in the beauty of a masterpiece without also sensing its significance is to experience a heady exaltation followed at once by a letdown, a feeling of frustration and emptiness. Aesthetics are not enough. Teachers who follow the present fashion of insisting that art be a "purely aesthetic" experience clip the wings of sensibility and cage the mind. They often discourage permanently the very people who thirst most after beauty, forcing true desire from the path.

Not even a sunset can be a "purely aesthetic" experience. Form and color say that the sun is in fact setting, that night is coming on and that the weather is shaping a certain way. "Red sun at night; sailors' delight." That saying shows beauty and significance joined as they always are. It also hints that the path of beauty is not restricted to connoisseurs. That path was part of Stone Age wisdom, and still is the main way for humanity. This is changing fast: factory and white-collar workers tread a way of ugliness. Yet most open-air workers keep, stumblingly or not, blindly or not, close to the path of beauty. And one in a thousand perhaps finds it a way beyond the seen.

Today the path of beauty is not much talked about. It sounds like a good thing for the luxuriously arty sort, and not for serious men. It is taken for a tortuous and mincing meander that skirts the ugly realities of life. The sorriest guide of all would be artiness, yet the path of beauty is often misunderstood, even among those who seek to follow it, for an epicurean or hedonistic carriage-road. Whole cultures have taken that Roman road straight off a cliff. Always certain sophisticates maintain that if only everything were in good taste war and ignorance might vanish.

They mistake the path of beauty as a way to beauty. It is not; it is a way through beauty.

And therefore it is really straight and plain. The finicky temper of the connoisseur is of all things most foreign to it. The man who finds a girl beautiful simply because she attracts him has only a dull animal sense of what beauty is. The same goes for the sophisticate who thinks a picture beautiful merely because it pleases him. It is well that he is pleased, of course, but it is not enough. Though his taste may be exquisite his sense of beauty remains unformed.

If one attempts to walk the path of beauty in a subjective, self-pampering mood, one's pleasures come to seem like slippery stepping-stones across a stream of pain. Finally one falls into the stream and drowns. The way lies not across the living and fatal stream, but into it. If one is ready the stream will carry him.

Why did the angel appear to the shepherds? Surely they were not wise, and Scripture says nothing about their being good. But these men slept breast to breast with the heavens; they were on the path of beauty. So too were the fishermen whom Christ Himself first called. In Duccio's *Calling of Peter and Andrew* at the National Gallery, the Apostles-to-be are bearded, careworn and yet children. Mindless they look, tugging at miracles upon the deep. Christ quietly, like a friend, beckons to them from the shore. For Peter and Andrew as for Duccio, the path of beauty lies through Him.

One need not be a Christian to find such pictures spiritually enlivening. The fact assumes particular importance in nonreligious times. Thus unbelieving Romans found spiritual help in the already ancient masterpieces of Greek statuary. Thus godless princes of the Renaissance encouraged fructifying genius. The present age—despite its few religious men and multitudinous lip-servers—is also non-religious. Science, not spirit, rules. Therefore, once again the spiritually athirst are turning to the path of beauty.

The way is hard to find just now. The science-pervaded mind fights shy of it. Those who tread the way seldom speak. Guides are few, and incline to be cultish. Cares are many, and every care a side-path. Indeed, the path of beauty is far more often lost than found.

When one has lost the path of beauty, one is sick. The main purpose of primitive art was to help heal such sickness. Indeed this healing quality is the floor of all art. Without this, art would be mere tickling, delusion, fraud. Matisse was recasting an ancient truth in modern terms when he said his pictures were meant to be like comfortable armchairs for the tired businessman.

Armchairs are not enough, however. Any art that strives merely for the healing beauties of the primitive, without its significance, is as transitional as a brief, dream-haunted nap. Modern art has recaptured something of the primitives' purity. It inhabits a world as fresh and clean as it is ancient; the world of spirit-forms. Yet so often it denies these forms' significance.

Therefore Australian Bushmen, African idol-whittlers and sand-painting Navajos still do best. Their forms and colors fit in a live way, as finger fits trigger. For all their strangeness and complexity nothing is blurred or unclear. This ebony mask makes a fist, being both at once. This sanded square becomes a shallow pool for spirits.

Such things are precise as blueprints and alive as flames. Simply to appreciate their beauty is like stepping out of the copyist's damp and dirty clothes into pure air. To study their significance as well can light the air with prophecy and hope.

The Navajo Indians have scant use for good deeds or truth-seeking. Instead they shape their lives to an ideal *hozojii,* the path of beauty. Art and song are their chief means to this shaping—Stone Age art and song.

Finding the tribe indomitable, Spanish colonists nicknamed it "Bloody Knives": hence "Navajo." They call themselves *Dineh,* meaning "Red Ant People." The nature of ants is to be numerous, industrious, orderly and strong: so an ant race would make formidable warriors. But ants are also of the earth, mysterious, set apart. These qualities also the Navajos reflect. Their old-time raids were always closely followed by purification rites. In peace these Myrmidons are gentle and austere. They use their purification ceremony still, right after graduation from the white man's compulsory schools. War, learning, life itself are ruled by the way for them; the way is the path of beauty.

Their guide to the path is a "medicine man," who combines in himself the professions of medicine, magic and priesthood with that of art. His entire method and belief date back to Stone Age culture. Therefore one greets him with some trepidation, as an ancestor older than Moses, or Lao-tse. He gazes into and through one's eyes, slowly, as if walking in imagination through unknown country. He says that the gods gave his ancestors painted buckskins as archetypes, never to be copied except in perishable materials. Perishable means more alive.

Though the gods took back the magic buckskins the medicine men remembered, and taught their sons. This happened long ago, when people were just beginning. Yet ever since then the medicine men have gone on re-creating the many, many pictures of the gods, exactly as they always were. One learns in youth. The pictures bring the gods. Far harder is learning to sing to the gods when they approach.

Clean yellow sand must first be found, a powdery charcoal, pollen for white, ground sandstone red. These pigments will be sown flat from the fist. Beneath his thumb the sand falls fine as hair. He makes a narrow rainbow facing east with head and feet at its tips. This rainbow goddess is to guard the gods to come. Hour by hour they take shape within the rainbow; they are tall, tall and weirdly narrow: their trunks like trees, their limbs tiny, their heads round or square. Lightning and corn, long cords and medicine bags are in their tiny hands. Side by side they speak together.

This family of gods, is it lying flat upon the yellow sand, or standing? Is it dancing, Indian-file, or motionless? No matter: the world here pictured is neither two nor three dimensioned, neither in motion nor at rest. It is that border world between the motions and dimensions of our own. The gods approach their picture; the medicine man rises from his knees.

The man who ordered the ceremony now comes forward. Hopefully he steps onto the sand-painting; he sits down amongst the gods. To show his reverence he eats a little of the sand. The medicine man is singing, asking the gods why they sent sickness to this man. At length they answer through the song. The sick man had stepped on a red ant by mistake; thus he offended. Yet this meeting is good; he will be forgiven; now he is forgiven and will soon be healed.

The stars are fading as the song goes on. The patient has been re-admitted to the path of beauty: beauty above him, beauty below him, beauty all around him, beauty all inside him. The ceremony ends. The medicine man destroys his picture. He would no more leave it running, so to speak, than an X-ray machine.

Now the gods have gone. Probably the patient will die. Yet he may have been given a breather. All patients die sooner or later, it seems, no matter how good the song or how handy the well-scrubbed fellow in the white gown. Ninety-nine times in a hundred, men leave the hospital walking. The hundredth time, no.

This lean, still, sunrise man crouching in bluejeans to scatter his picture with an eagle feather, has brought home gods to a soul. Instead of molding nature, like a sorcerer or scientist, he remolds human nature. By songs and images he keeps closing the rift that keeps on opening between one man and all creation.

Bernard Berenson once spent an afternoon contemplating Chinese drawings of wintry landscapes. Rising at last to go, he saw the museum window filled with snowy dusk. "That," he exclaimed, pointing to the window, "is the best of all!" Berenson's own center had shifted from himself to the pictures. The drawings before him had ceased to be a delectation in themselves and become the means of experiencing further beauty. This might be thought a personal achievement but its cause lay outside him. All un consciously, Berenson had put himself in the Chinese artists' place. He saw the window with the eyes of the men who made the drawings. In fact those far-distant and long-dead artists had joined to create a new picture for Berenson in the snow.

When great art is so deeply felt and understood, it ceases to be a collection of beautiful objects and becomes instead a succession of gateways. And whenever this happens art reveals the path of beauty. Thus philosophy can reveal the path of wisdom, and Christ the path of loving kindness.

Such are the ideal paths: beauty, wisdom and loving kindness. They relate, of course, to faith, hope and charity. It may be less obvious that they also relate to the three phases of human accomplishment, which are desire, thought, and action. They lend freedom to each phase. Choosing in itself is nothing much; consider the dope addict. Only on the paths of beauty, wisdom and loving kindness is any true freedom possible. In fact the only free desire is a beautiful desire—a desire for something worth choosing. Likewise the only free thought is a wise thought and the only free act is a good act.

The path of beauty comes first of all this—and like the smell of coffee in the morning it makes a fine start.

A masterpiece of Memling's at Munich has the Three Kings in its center foreground adoring Christ and the same Kings keeping separate vigil on three mountains in the background. This enormously complex little picture repeats the figures again and again, comic-strip style, to tell their entire stories. The Three Kings come down from their mountains, join in following the Star, meet Herod, worship the Child and return by boat. Their journey is a flat loop through the composition. Crossing Herod's smaller loop it causes the Massacre of the Innocents. It just touches the life of Christ, which unfolds across the foreground. However, the place where the Magi take ship lies close by Emmaus. And there a hound who had made the whole pilgrimage with the Kings leaves them and crosses over into the other story.

Traditionally the Magis' path was one of wisdom. Memling makes it a path of beauty first of all. At the point of meeting Christ it becomes a path of loving kindness also. Memling's picture merges the three possible paths.

The path of beauty compasses a thousand sacred places and a thousand thousand altars—some ephemeral and others built deep as the hills.

Yet as mankind evolves, the path grows ever more precarious. It was already harder for the Navajo medicine man than for his fellows and it is harder for artists always—not harder to follow but more dangerous to fall from. To lose the path, once consciously gained, is agony, like loss of reason. And to regain the path can be equally painful, like regaining life in a frozen limb.

Or it may be like the conversion of Saint Paul, a single searing stroke. No man may ride directly and at once up to such lightning, so Saint Paul must have trod the path of beauty before, on pre-Christian heights. But he had never been so smashed and re-shaped to the path as now. The moment of Paul's conversion has been a welcome challenge to great artists because so many of them understand how inspiration can crack and burn the heart. In Michelangelo's volcanic vision at the Vatican, Paul sprawls licked and tumbled with terror, like a bear cub half-shaped.

Bruegel's version at Vienna is on the contrary as peaceful and shaded as a high-hidden nest. And yet, to see this picture is first of all to join Paul's armed expedition. One is crossing a mountain range close to the sky. Down the trail, beside a still grove, somebody lies unhorsed—apparently the captain. Part of the column ahead of him turns back at the news. Another part continues on a curving path that will eventually lead around by the grove again. Meanwhile one's comrades in the rear are pressing forward down the path, hoping to learn more of this. Invisibly, amongst an army, one moves down the path of beauty toward a still grove, a stricken saint, and lightning.

Chapter 14

Gifts for the Gods

IN ALL THE SWARMING VISIONS OF HIERONYMUS Bosch, one figure stands out heroically: the Black King in his *Nativity,* at the Prado. While the other Magi kneel he waits erect before his infant Lord, not proudly but with vital calm. The youngest of the Kings, he is also the most gorgeously attired, but instead of the trappings of church or state he wears the slashed and shining white robes of contemplation, whose tassels trail the ground like spring rain. One feels he must have been the first to see the Star of Bethlehem. Himself a darkness at rest on the wide darkness, he looked up and saw the light.

Though never a mere instrument of organized religion, great art is always an in-pouring of spiritual light. Therefore one who dares to interpret it must also explore religion, and behind religion, myth. He can treat all myths and religions whatsoever as fact, as having happened, irrevocably, in human consciousness.

One speaks of religious art, but great art is always religious—in the individual and not the institutional sense of of the word. The nature of great art is to convey spiritual truths. Nobody pretends that such truths are to be found only in church, or in the Bible. The Bible itself is a work of art, and art also is a Bible.

Who still worships the Great Goddess of Mycenaean times? And yet her bust at the Prado lives on, radiating life. Also, to see the true Greek statues is to step back for a moment into the sunlight of a time when men were so familiar with their gods as to recognize them naked. The sculptors died with their gods. The marble lives—and shines with spiritual truth. Even to see the truth of it is just a beginning.

Bruegel's *Massacre of the Innocents* at Vienna is like a falling down into darkness from light, falling, whirling and melting like snow. People are not apt to pause very long before this picture. The details of murder and bereavement are so plain and so terrible. Bruegel has heaped up horrors like dishes upon the smiling snow. One despairs, finally, and turns to escape. But there is no escaping this picture. It will remain a place of suffering inside one's mind until one goes back to look at it again.

There is an empty nest in a tree overlooking the scene. Apparently the birds have flown. Bruegel was fond of such plain analogies, which both underscored his meanings and masked the profundity of his thoughts. Escape lies not outside the picture but inside. One finds it with a kind of new-born joy. For although the soldiers are breaking into the stable and searching—just as oneself has been doing, without knowing what one sought—He is fled.

One's own escape lies through the picture and out again, with Christ. He has fled that mindless, heartless slaughter, and yet now He is here, in one's own mind and heart.

The eye of imagination is dark and yet it fills with light, both from within and from without. *I am dark, but comely.* In so many European churches, the chapel of the Black Virgin has the freshest flowers. The Black Virgin of Montserrat, the spiritual mother of all Catalonia, sits at the heart of the sawed mountain, dark as onyx and outer space. Like light and will upon the lap of fate, Christ sits erect upon her knee.

My mother bore me in the southern wild,
And I am dark, but oh, my soul is white!

Glancing straight at the sun, a man sees darkness only. Somebody standing between him and the sun—closer to the light—will also appear dark. Religious art often seems to be a darkness in itself—polished obscurity—as all official art is apt to be. But when the greatest art of any faith appears obscure it is because it stands as a welcome before the light.

"Thou shalt have no other gods before me!" Jehovah said. "Thou shalt make unto thee no graven image. . . ." For all that, most of mankind keeps on making images and a good half tries to picture God. The difficulties—especially in giving body to such philosophical constructions as the Holy Trinity—are inconceivable, let alone surmountable. Yet man must have images. To illustrate the Trinity, Saint Patrick picked a shamrock.

El Greco's pictures are like ephemeral wax matches lifted to illuminate unheard-of chapels. Some he designed for actual chapels, as sacred spaces inside sacred places. For these, El Greco followed Tintoretto's lead in sculpting clay models first. He would place the model at just the same angle from which his picture was to be viewed, and then paint from it. This technical consideration explains away the charge of "astigmatism" that is so often brought against him. One has only to kneel down before El Greco's *Nativity* at the Prado to see its so-called distortions vanish. One gazes up into a tilted, flamelike cone.

Many other masterpieces of religious art that were painted to be seen from below now hang at eye-level in museums—confusingly enough. The foreground of Mantegna's *Crucifixion* at the Louvre seems to fall away without cause. But if one takes the trouble to gaze up at the picture from a kneeling position one finds oneself in an open grave at the foot of the Cross, as was intended. The only way to join the worshipers in Bruegel's *Nativity,* at the National Gallery in London, is to kneel before it. Finally, the van Eycks' *Holy Lamb,* at Ghent, appears to be loose and strange in composition until one kneels down, and then it becomes a broad staircase to heaven.

The painted vaults of Byzantine and Romanesque art require another kind of seeing in motion: they swell and spin as one walks under them.

Ancient Greek vases need to be turned in the hand. Red-figured Greek bowls, black and shallow, ought to be gazed into from a sipping position—as from the rim of sleep. Such ceramics served to spread the Greek religion all around the Mediterranean coast. They gained power from being used.

Religious art is all one and all different. It may be that El Greco—a Cretan and by turns three kinds of Catholic—Orthodox, Roman and Spanish—was in truth the last of the Uranus-worshipers. To the ancient Cretans Uranus was Father Sky, who rained his seed upon Mother Earth. These two created and ruled all, until their son Cronus grew up, castrated Uranus with a flint sickle, and flung his genitals into the sea. From the foam of Uranus' genitals was Aphrodite born.

What all this means is anybody's guess. One may even choose to believe that Cronus was the rebellious god of astronomer-priests. Until astronomy, Father Sky remained an indecipherable swirl of blaze and dark, the darkness filled with eyes, or with the seeds of far-off life, burning and twinkling everywhere afar. Doubtless one of his night-names was Argus, the Hundred-Eyed, keeper of Io, the White Cow, which is the horned moon. By day he made the sun impregnate Mother Earth, with hot archery; he made the cool soft archery of the rain leap down to her. By night he flung down stars, sometimes, and trailed his constellations in the shivering sea. Was he not mighty? Who could stand against him?

Only Cronus, meaning time, and measurement. That frightening flint sickle may even have been a star-plotting device. Once men could measure and predict the movements of the stars—once they knew, for example, that Orion is drowned for two months every spring—they knew as well that Father Sky is not all-powerful but owes obedience to time.

> *When the stars threw down their spears*
> *And watered heaven with their tears . . .*

The dying Uranus prophesied that Cronus in turn would be dethroned by his own children. Therefore Cronus swallowed them one by one—a way time has. Only Zeus escaped by trickery and then returned to conquer Cronus and banish him to Britain. There the old god still rules; his seat is at Greenwich. And as the master of all measurement, which is science, Cronus has waxed young and strong once more.

What of Uranus, Father Sky, great-grandfather of the gods; did he really die? Not likely. Yet to see the stars with a cold eye is to castrate him again. Artists might have helped men see the stars better. But how to represent the chill burning, the steady twinkle, the illimitable nearness, and torrential order of the stars? No, it is impossible.

Therefore El Greco brought the stars to earth. He formed saints and Madonnas of them. Christian saints and Madonnas, true, yet formed of the foam of the seed of Father Sky—*when all the sons of heaven shouted for joy.* The thunder of their shout sounds throughout El Greco. So many of his canvases are like a tall, dark-silver gong, flashing, ringing, crackling, roaring, singing, humming under an unseen blow.

El Greco's canvases are curiously hard to recall separately —except for a few of the more conventional ones such as the *Burial of Count Orgaz.* His greatest are like a succession of nights alone on a raft under the stars; they merge in memory, and the night sky is what best brings them back. Especially the night sky of Spain, over the high central plateau. El Greco lived under this same sky. His house at Toledo, with its eye of a patio, stands gazing still at the sky. His garden sloped athwart the sky to the high cliff of the River Tagus. Below the hills draw up their knees like women under the starlit sheets.

El Greco's figures appear between earth and sky: yearning, leaping, soaring, descending. Their proportions are not regular, nor small nor large, nor human, even; they defy measurement. The space they soar is vast and yet immediate. One can almost embrace it, like hugging the sky to one's face. There is no depth in the measured sense; one passes from near to far in a flash. The limbs cannot be grasped, no more than fire; burning they twist away. The lips are speaking to someone else; the eyes look away and aloft. Light has a jagged edge, and shadow shines at its core. The colors well like bloodstains from within; or they blaze out, suddenly. All is constellations interlocked and many-pointed, flat yet afar, cold yet ablaze and very near.

El Greco must have studied the stars, not as objects but as signs, as letters to be combined. If the cave men saw animals in fire-shadows, if Leonardo saw men in wall-cracks and stains, El Greco found his saints and angels amongst the stars, in the spaces between the stars. He painted them so. It is nothing new to imagination. The ancients peopled the heavens and we can as well.

To see Orion in the sky with his bow, is hard, and yet how rewarding! It is to see Orion. El Greco saw him too, doubtless, and all the rest besides. Then he went on to the still harder task—harder for adults if not for children—of finding new combinations of star-signs, new sons of Father Sky. Finally he did the impossible, bringing these new creations down from the sky and making them real in art. They carry the sky with them, not only in their wings and eyes but even in their knees and elbows, their navels and their beards and fingertips. They breathe the dark pure breath of Uranus.

Having come down to earth they leap up and away again—messengers between the Earth and Sky.

Christ is king of this heavenly host. In El Greco's *Crucifixion,* at the Louvre, Christ in His torment seems close to wrenching the Cross right up out of the parched earth. In the blind moment when the heart stops, a brightness rising on the black wave, outstretched, He returns to the Father.

Chapter 15

An End to Subject-Matter

ABSTRACTIONISM IS OF COURSE THE CHIEF CHARacteristic of twentieth-century art. Practically all the moderns use abstraction. A few laymen profess to understand it, and yet for the vast majority abstract art remains an irritating mystery. Need this be so?

There is no "explaining" abstract art—or any other kind, for that matter. Art cannot be reasoned out; it must be seen into. Still, one may explore the territory of the abstractionists. It is not a part of the moon but of this world, and borders everywhere on common ground.

Until the last hundred years or so, thought was understood to be the ruling force of art: conception ruled the forms. There were exceptions, of course, even among the masters. Vermeer, for example, seems to abdicate intellectual control in favor of some other power. But the vast majority of masterpieces are so by virtue of some clear conception, which puts their execution in the shade. Indeed the old masters often left to apprentices the detailed execution of their ideas. No stronger proof could be desired for the fact, now largely forgotten, that they put mind-sight over eye-sight.

Picasso does too, and shows it in his own arbitrary fashion by painting carelessly. When someone asked him how he had the nerve to produce pictures that would begin to fade, crack and fall apart the moment they left his easel, he replied, "It is the legend that lives." What he meant was "the thought."

However, the fact is that between Goya and Picasso—those two black-spirited and philosophic Spaniards—thought went out of art. Men kept on painting ideas as before, but life and true significance had fled. Strange, after so many centuries, yet there it was: an ebb-tide. Like all ebb-tides it held a promise. The time had come for a newly active and honest art, far removed from the now darkened fields of contemplation.

Perhaps there is no such thing as a new idea, or a new form either. But there is such a thing as a new approach, which combines the two.

This the French impressionists provided. They raised a new challenge: to picture, by means of rapidly dabbed colors alone, the play of actual sunlight over the earth. Mental visualization could be no use to so intense, immediate and athletic an attempt as this—which might be compared to painting the stripes on a moving tiger. Its accomplishment required a complete shift of emphasis, from drawing to color, from visualization to execution and, most important, from mind-sight to eye-sight.

Impressionism, that rainbow gateway to modern art, was anything but illustrative, symbolic or overtly meaningful. By avoiding preconception, by leaping straight into the making of a picture, and by disavowing all overt significance the impressionists anticipated pure abstractionism —which also does these things.

All that remained was to eliminate subject-matter as well. This process the post-impressionists, *fauves* and German expressionists began, only piecemeal. They held on to subject-matter in a general way while at the same time doing ecstatic violence to its details—painting a sky-blue oak tree against an orange sky, or an impossibly twisted mistress with chartreuse hair and lemon-lidded eyes. Sometimes for emotive power and sometimes for decorative appeal, they willingly sacrificed not the real world exactly, but the sense of it.

Merely decorative art might be defined as pleasing but insignificant. Merely expressive art is pointed but unpleasant. In general the semi-abstractionists have balanced off these possibilities by painting the stripes without the tiger. The stripes are handsome and surprising in themselves, they give pleasure in themselves, and yet they do still hint at tigerness, at the splendors and terrors of the tiger.

So the way to abstractionism, as to all new forms, was prepared by sacrifice: first the sacrifice of all overt significance and then, piecemeal, the sacrifice of subject-matter. Such sacrifices had been made before, of course, but never on this universal scale. Crivelli long ago practiced semi-abstraction for the sake of decorative aplomb, but it took the School of Paris to make this a standard practice.

If semi-abstract art has always pointed a path toward pure abstractionism, why was not the path explored long ago? The answer is that it appeared to lead downhill. The Venetians considered Giovanni Bellini a bigger man than Crivelli. To sacrifice the sense of reality to mere decoration, they believed, is to begin a descent toward the artisans' quarter.

The apples and other fruits in Crivelli's paintings come disguised. He intended them to look like fruits carved out of precious stones, and so they do. In Braque's still-lifes, the fruits are intended to be seen as paint, as parts of the painting itself. They may resemble fruits at first glance but this resemblance shortly fades to an allusion, or else a distillation, like applejack.

In either case the apple's appleness is sacrificed, deliberately, to the painting's paintingness. As readily as a general sacrifices lives to victory will a Crivelli or a Braque sacrifice the representation of life to design. Not so Cézanne, for example. Much has been written about the abstract qualities of his art, and they are there, yet reality is there too, swept up into the canvas and firmly embraced. Crivelli's apples harden into stone and Braque's soften into paint before one's eyes: Cézanne's get juicier and juicier.

Genius can weave life and art, representation and design, into a single fabric. Therefore, Bellini and his pupils, Titian and Giorgione, denied none of it. They knew of no forbidden fruit: life brought everything to them, it seemed, and they in turn brought life to everything. Let the minor masters make the sacrifices! Genius smiled and strode on.

Men of genius from the Renaissance to Cézanne had, or thought they had, good reason for not exploring the path towards abstractionism. Yet when at last in the twentieth century the abstract path began to be explored it was found to lead elsewhere than expected. Instead of descending all the way to the artisans' quarter it took a sharp turn upward, towards the citadel of the mystics.

The pure abstractionists have sacrificed the tiger altogether. He is consumed: hide, entrails, teeth, everything. Content—manifest content—has been wholly burned away. Where, then, can significance reside? Is not mere decoration, meaningless now, the foregone result?

One hears of "pure forms" but what are they? A pure form presumably would be a shape in space having a certain color and consistency and nothing more. It would possess neither seed nor skin, neither any precedents nor the least and most ephemeral associations. To make such a form would be a miracle, surely, like producing absolute zero.

Purism need not exclude representation. Van der Weyden set white lilies against Gabriel's white robe, and kept the loveliness of each. The point about purism is that it can only go so far. To paint a white square against a white canvas may be closer to abstraction than van der Weyden was, but not to "pure form."

Decorative stabs in the direction of pure forms might be to paint a turtle crimson or give plate-lips to Ubangi girls. The turtle and the lips no longer look like themselves, yet something of their nature will shine through. Artificial forms come closer, especially when accident removes them from the world of use. There is a certain purity about an empty gas pump, which can be damned annoying too. The R.C.A. Building would, if it lacked elevators, have a monumental purity. The simpler the purer: a cut gem seen by a color-blind man, a doghouse blanketed in snow, a frozen wash-cloth or a spoon without a handle. Or, finally, a painted fragment of a pattern, as in Mondrian.

There are no pure forms. One cannot see with the eye alone. The mind cooperates and confers significance on what one sees. To gaze upon a Mondrian is to think of many things, in time. Linoleum comes first, ironically, since he inspired linoleum patterns and not the reverse. An object that seems to lack associations will itself create them soon enough.

The manifest content of a Vermeer represents something he saw, and yet the picture's latent content, its true significance, transcends representation alone. In pure abstractions the manifest content is effaced, but perhaps the latent content will appear.

Mondrian's pictures are almost impossible to recall exactly. But this is nothing against him; it might be said of Vermeer as well. Was that small blue square in the Mondrian an inch from the top, or closer to an inch and a quarter? How many chimneys are there in Vermeer's *View of Delft?*

Is it fair to compare Mondrian with the immortal Vermeer? Why not? Mondrian is perhaps the greatest champion of abstract art, and champions require testing—the more severe the better.

The stillness of these two Dutchmen is fabulous, and so is their elusiveness. Both were mystical, concerned with something "other," something outside of what they painted. This is what makes their pictures so still, as if waiting in the summer noon, and so hard to remember. One seems to remember something which was not there. One recalls not a picture so much as a state of being—of being held calm and still.

Mondrian's art has been a cleansing wind and yet it carries, just as surely as he was born, the breath of what he was born to: old Dutch cleanliness, dikes and faith in dikes. It is as exact as an ideal expense account, with no padding and no mistakes. If it were business it would be good business.

Like his country, Mondrian's pictures are small without being humble, and severe without aggressiveness. They are like ideal though humorless communities of squares and straight-men, where each part keeps its place and is serene. Cheerful, even, for there is a certain bright cheer in Mondrian as in a china cabinet. In short, there never was a more bourgeois, just, pat, dry, nor altogether Dutch artist. Even his pictures are Dutch treat: one brings what one can or goes hungry.

One cannot walk around in a Vermeer, as in more illusionistic art, nor can one concentrate for long on its design, as with some abstractions. He paints a third world somewhere between surface and story, guarded well, as in a crystal castle. Peer as one will at his very paint, it clings neither to imaginary surfaces nor to the physical one, but somewhere between. One is peering into depths of crystal. Like Mondrian, Vermeer approached this third world by a process of rejection. He kept rejecting everything that was not there. He never told a fib in the interest of the picturesque. He neither added nor subtracted chimneys in his *View of Delft*.

Vermeer kept rejecting the world of his imagination until it came back naked and invisible, to stay forever, storyless and impossible to grasp. It is not so much a mystery—this third world—as a non-mystery. It cannot be understood and yet it makes itself understood.

Music—which is another kind of sorcery—can demonstrate the possibility of this. For instance, Beethoven hardly pauses to please the ear; he plunges straight down through the world of sound to enter the silent, undersea palace of the soul. Blake's best poems also do this: the words are unheard. Vermeer could reach the soul with pictures.

Vermeer's *The Letter* at Amsterdam can be opened at first glance yet never read through. There is a pregnant girl standing before a map and reading a letter. Perhaps the letter came from her husband; perhaps he is a sea captain far away. Will he get back in time for her lying-in? Who is he, anyway? And here the picture swells and blurs. Who is she? Who will her child be? Is this another kind of Annunciation?

Afterwards, one begins to hear one's own heart beating. Or is it her heart, or the captain's, or the unborn baby's heart? The composition forms a whirling sun-disk, with the hidden embryo at its center. The alternating light and dark squares of the design beat and beat around the hidden center, like heart-beats.

In Mondrian also the center is hidden: he generally keeps it as white and bare as snowfields in Holland. Around the center Mondrian constructs an off-beat rhythm of squares like tulip-patches and straight lines intersecting like the Dutch canals. Whatever lies beneath the snowy, checkered tablecloth of Mondrian's pictures remain as unknowable as the letter in the hand of Vermeer's model.

Vermeer had left out everything except what he could see. Mondrian did just the opposite: he left out everything that he could actually see.

Yet a man is always a creature of space as well as time, and Mondrian's empty-seeming art is packed full of his native Holland. The Low Countries consist mainly of two flat planes—earth and sky—at right angles. Mondrian's pictures are also horizontal or vertical or both at once. One cannot make them slope or undulate. The reflections in the Amsterdam canals are Rembrandt-brown, but the ranked façades that they reflect are white, black, red, blue and yellow. Façades of lines and squares in primary colors —that describes both Mondrian's art and the view from an Amsterdam canal boat.

He never painted a world remote. His mysteries, like Vermeer's, concern the here-and-now—the unknown, nestling, strange to touch, in the familiar pocket of the known, or the invisible at the street corner.

Mondrian's method was to rule out all the warm adornments of the seen world: all the curves, and sunny heights, and smudges and surprises, all the sparkling, dreaming disarray of nature, her million moods and ways, with a brand-new dress for each. To deny all that seems grim and yet the alchemists' gold-making methods were the same: burning, boiling, rotting, distilling almost everything away. The physicist, clawing and banging at his atom, is another such puritan. He digs for unknown principles within the here-and-now.

An absolutely pure act, such as the alchemists attempted and physicists approximate in their vacuum-chambers, has got to be the pure manifestation of a principle, carried over into the world of process. This may be, strictly speaking, impossible. Yet most good men do attempt it somehow at some time in their lives, and when they do they come closest to godliness. For example, heroes in battle are storming this height; they carry principle past the jaws of death. Mystics do the same at certain moments. So do lovers, and artists.

Not pure forms but pure acts are the abstract artist's goal.

Abstractions, then, should not be seen as pictures but as acts. They are young cousins to that legendary Chinese calligraph, a masterpiece ecstatically scrawled on the wall of a house, reading "I am drunk!" This only says that the artist was in another state than that of the man looking at the picture. One man's drink is another man's ambrosia.

And to find the meaning is to forget the message.

Chapter 16

The Way of Abstract Expression

IN MONDRIAN, ABSTRACT PAINTING HAD A STRAIT-laced mother. Kandinsky was its father, so to speak. As against careful geometric balancings, he stood for trapezes, fire and flux. Indeed his first abstractions were landscapes fused and melted down by the force of his emotions while painting. One can still discern a stray cloud or a tree or a cannon floating sometimes near the surfaces of these ecstatic oils.

Kandinsky was fond of comparing art to music and both to philosophy. He tried to formulate a system wherein forms and colors would have certain definite relationships, like notes in music, and also philosophic meanings. This was too systematic to succeed. But his idea of improvising freely, like a jazz musician with paints, has had enormous influence.

Even the most daring and wild abstractionists now living go back to Kandinsky, just as the most daring and severe go back to Mondrian. No harm here. In walking, the feet go backward as well as forward.

Among Mondrian's followers, Josef Albers is even more

austere. Albers paints precisely the same composition of squares within squares over and over again, changing only the colors. It is as if Albers were not painting pictures at all but square nests of colors. They have no bulk, however, nor are they flat—because his colors will not stay still. His colors pulse, glance, darken, and keep changing like ripples from a stone tossed into a still pool. Their emanations—unpainted and yet present to the eye—are mainly circular.

The square is a specifically human construction, rarely found in the world of nature. It is both confining and confined—rigid, exact, intellectual. The circle is opposite to all this. Albers always moves from the square towards the circle, seeking to include the natural perfection of the second within the intellectual perfection of the first. Since everybody tries to do the same thing in himself—to include naturalness within rightness—Albers' art is humanistic. There is a tendency to say that humanistic painting must contain human figures, but why? Since human thought is itself an abstracting process, there is no basic conflict between abstraction and humanism.

As thought can be full of feeling, so forms can be full of color. And just as feeling can modify thought, so color can modify forms. With forms that well with color, Albers makes a new approach to an ancient metaphysical problem —squaring the circle. To square the circle thus is like mastering things without moving. One bends the straight and straightens the bent without so much as a touch. It is a question of experiencing color within form, heart within thought, and naturalness within rightness.

The present age happens to be very strong on the externals of such experience—on form, thought and rightness in themselves alone. It is the time of the crustaceans, the hard-shelled scientists. In protest against this state of things the abstract expressionists—Kandinsky's heirs—have parted company with the heirs of Mondrian. This is no time, they believe, for ideal balancings: this is the time to rebel against externals, break them up, discard them, and fight back through to the inner core—which consists in color alone, heart alone, freedom alone.

It may be objected that colors, at least, are themselves externals, belonging not to the forms but to exterior light. An orange is not orange—just a round fruit that happens to reflect orange light. In optics, this holds. It also holds for a good deal of art. Leonardo would have had no difficulty in accepting it. With modern art the case is very different. Most painters now begin with colors. Hence, colors are their raw material. Their colors underlie the forms. To scientists, structure is basic. To painters, color can be basic.

By making this much plain, impressionism changed the course of art. Chiaroscuro retreated into history before a new blaze of color. Then Cézanne showed how to actually build with colors. But the abstract expressionists have no wish to follow Cézanne in this regard. They are consistent in sacrificing form—a crystallization—to color, the primal stuff. Their colors are woven, so to speak, into a fluid and indefinite fabric, roughly on a plane with the canvas beneath. Rising, reeling, spreading, their colors display an unsuspected and as yet practically formless power.

My kid could do better than that!

This universal objection to abstract expressionist art carries weight. Given half a chance, children under twelve could easily put up a better show. Their colors are more daring, contours more buoyant, shapes more surprising and compositions more alive—naturally.

Since this kind of painting is first of all a relatively free action, it ought to be expected that children perform it best. They run best also, their feet barely skimming the ground. They sleep best. They laugh and cry best. They play best, as a rule. And all because in doing these things they are not burdened with ideas. Thought, like flesh, is something of a burden: children have less of both, and good for them. Their souls are freer. This should not discourage adults but inspire them.

Adults must try to be natural—a pathetic and yet necessary contradiction. Otherwise they will become unnatural, and die before their bodies. If artists tend to stay youthful it is because they so often strive to get back through youth to the clarity of childhood vision. The abstract expressionists in particular boast of not even knowing what they are about. Is this true, or is it a little extravagant? Coleridge wrote "Kubla Khan" in a drugged trance. And yet in general he kept thinking hard. All the great creators appear to have been thinkers—at least in their leisure time. And if there are masters of abstract expressionism this will doubtless hold for them as well.

Meanwhile the abstract expressionists are playing with colors, passionately and as it were unthinkingly. To play is their way inward, and the fewer rules the better. It is like a game of cowboys-and-Indians that draws these artists home from the numbered streets, in through the tall grass of the corner lot. Watching the game from the street, one may see only ripplings in the tall grass—green, yellow, blue, brown: colors sharp and thick. Sometimes this corner prairie appears to be on fire, and perhaps it is.

The people most involved in abstract expression can get pretty fiery--which comes as a shock. One expects artists of the stature of Willem de Kooning and Jackson Pollock to reach out instead of striking out. The violence of their art has been called a kind of protest against public apathy, but this does not satisfy. One might table the fact that the violence is assuredly there together with the fact that abstract expressionism commands a large and passionate huddle of supporters.

Granted that most people care not a hoot for abstract expression, this apathy faces all of painting now like a wall. Art has slipped its accustomed mooring in the harbor of civilized thought and silently drifted out to sea. Who is to blame for this? "Modern artists," the cry goes up, "and especially abstractionists who don't want to be understood!"

How can a man be sure of understanding, let alone expressing, the true qualities of any abstract picture? Today's methods, which consist almost exclusively of analyzing the composition and providing a few polite analogies, are limited. The news that such-and-such an abstract painting includes a number of diagonals which may possibly reflect the cold war, must be cold comfort to a man who sincerely wants to get inside the picture and cannot. The more intelligent he is the more will he feel excluded and put off by such supposed aids. The truth is that abstract art, like all art, is a matter of personal experience. Being "sure" has not got much to do with it.

The abstract expressionists have special ways of demanding that their pictures be experienced and not just looked at. First, they make much of their brush strokes; instead of concealing the painting process—as would a smooth realist—they dramatize it. This helps persuade one to view abstract expressionist art within an imaginary time sequence. One paints the picture over again in the mind's eye. This time-dimension substitutes for the usual space-dimension, which is reduced to an uncertain surface.

Imagine a long and often illegible letter scrawled out over page after crumpled page through the midnight hours. Follow that with a brief, careful recapitulation, neatly typed in the cool of the dawn. Will not the first version carry more emotion? The abstract expressionists stop, on purpose, at the first version.

There are exceptions: Matthieu's brushmanship is more classy than frenzied, and Soulage makes smears neat. Mark Rothko's melting dawn-stripes are insistent only by reason of their extraordinary size. Such hugeness as Rothko's has become a constant in abstract expressionist painting. The purpose again is to involve the viewer. An easel-picture can be taken in—though not experienced—at a single glance, while a wall-sized canvas cannot.

The abstract expressionist enlarges his canvas on the same principle that makes a lover write his letters long. And like the lover he has faith that he can communicate directly. Communicate what? Self, they say.

But what is the self trying to express? Itself, purely.

What is this pure self? Has it no definable attributes? None, perhaps.

In that case it is not the self at all; it is the soul, and the abstract expressionist's yearning is not so much to express as to possess it. But such possessing involves a terrible adventure, inward across a ring of fire. And this is really what explains the violence of abstract expressionism. Feeling and thinking are a man's means of moving outward from himself. When he turns and tries to move inward all the way to his own still center, his senses and his intellect alike blaze up, denying him admission.

The self is not at the center. One must go in through the self, to find the soul. The fever of that journey!

An abstract masterpiece has got to be a pure and perfect action, ego-less, emanating from the still soul outward to the world again. Has this been accomplished in painting? If not yet, how great a triumph awaits!

Chapter 17

Art and Infinity

WHEN A WORK OF ART TRANSCENDS THE PLEASURE-giving function of a ball gown or a Music Hall show, wherein does it transcend? What lies beyond the principles of pain and pleasure?

Sickness can be even more frightening than painful, when it offers a glimpse of coming death. Health on the other hand is even more reassuring than pleasurable, when it offers a healing contact with the infinite and eternal.

Each man knows the shape of such a contact from his own experience. Orientals may be led to think of terraced temples, mandalas, and high porches of contemplation. A European Catholic may see the heaven-pointing spires of his town cathedral slowly rising as he motors home across the plain. Explorers of antiquity may think of Delphi, the Pass of the Throwing-down of the Moorish Dogs, Montserrat, and similar high places where a narrow gorge opens out finally and the rocks leap skyward.

Outward journeys can resemble inward ones: a pilgrimage is the blunt knight's prayer.

Driving to Granada, one crosses a high range of mountains where the people live in caves. Their doors and windows are like mouths and eyes. Granada is a deep coil of dazzling sunlight and shadow, serpentlike, surrounding the cool green Alhambra—the mountain of fountains that fans itself. Within the ring of mountain peaks lies the searing plain and within the plain coils white Granada and within Granada rises the green hill of the Alhambra and atop the hill hovers the Alcazar like a mirage, and to enter here is a withdrawal.

Patterns upon patterns snare one's gaze, interminable yet exuberant. In the high rooms they rise from house-of-cards constructions to skyrocket sprays and comets and, near the top, revolving, pulsating shapes like saucers of blossoms. The ceilings are shaped like the undersides of fountains and fountains spring up from the floors.

Said the angel to Mohammed: "Let your artists copy nothing, if they would serve God." So the Alcazar of the Alhambra is wholly abstract, except for the Eastern-seeming lions in its central court.

Looking out from it one believes in magic carpets. Then looking down into its garden pools one thinks of a straw mat floating upon the deep—or of the mind. When nature hints at eternity it is by opening outward—racing clouds witnessed from a waving treetop. When art does the same it is inward—the wind purpling a puddle. The Alhambra comes close to excluding nature: it is all inward. The alcoves and doors with fretted lids are like ears and eyes within which one withdraws, farther and farther. One withdraws from sense of touch, even, for the million tiles shine like color impalpable. Within, far within, these half-frozen and half-liquid domes, all closely patterned as transistor-sets, are like palaces of the unthought, inside one's own mind.

God, like death, needs no attributes. Nor does thought

have attributes, until it be thought. The Alhambra is a place patterned to the flowing of these imponderables.

One draws near the center, the court wherein four streams come together, rivers of Paradise, at a fountain guarded by stone lions in a circle. Why lions? Why creatures again, here at the creatureless heart? They are alert and still. It is painful to see them, wild beasts at home in a sacred place, a place removed. They are at home, however, like golden, circling, all-devouring time. From their cruel mouths flows cool water. Only to drink of this water, they say, thirsting, is to know eternal youth.

Nothing so subjectively refined as the Alhambra appeared in Christian architecture until Gothic times. Byzantine and Romanesque churches were places of holy communion, where faithful souls flocked together happily. The Gothic churches were to be places of contemplation, where doubting souls might spring, separately although together, into spiritual life.

The crossbow of the body: stone gloriously echoing and exalting our doomed flesh, just as music echoes and exalts our doomed minds: a building like a body and a crossbow, expressly designed to release the spirit into self-controlled free flight—Chartres Cathedral. Before the altar, one is where the arrow lays its neck upon the bow. Also one moves at the invisible heart of an invisible body: heart within heart, like Jonah in the whale's belly.

But suppose that one goes there coolly, not as a pilgrim, simply to gain pleasure, blameless pleasure? Even so one finds oneself at the same place before the altar. The eastward rush of columns has drawn one forward and now the transept opening outward and the nave opening upward invite one to halt. Looking straight up, one sees what might be a night sky dimly ribbed with constellations, and something inside of one longs to spring up there, like the tall windows that sift an other-worldly blaze. If the Alhambra hinted, with its hovering, at infinity below, Chartres, with its aspiring, hints at infinity above.

One is held for a moment in a tension between emphatically horizontal and emphatically vertical space. These forces are built into the stone and they really do tug at one, just as the Holland Tunnel seems to pull one forward and the R.C.A. Building to pull one upward.

In the dark, towering air of Chartres—in the stillness between two spatial chords, as it were—one's spirit sometimes arrows up and away in free, exultant flight. This can happen to anyone who comes there. The cathedral was built for the purpose, by men who knew exactly what they did.

Those who claim for architecture that it is the one art of actual space must have a limited idea of actuality. Reading *Moby Dick,* for example, one sails and sails and sails the seas in the *Pequod.* How actually spatial can you get? And is not music also spatial? Flamenco singing tumbles one down underground torrents of sound. Listening to Benny Goodman can be like a catnap on a wide, low, open bed set in the center of the North American prairie in the summer dusk, with black and silver notes beading the shadowy air. And when old Bach starts building his cathedrals in a soul—stone by note by stone by note—they rise from soft low country to Himalayas, and then take to snowy wing.

In my Father's house are many mansions. Paintings, too, are mansions of the soul.

There is as much space inside a person's soul as there

is outside. Infinity works both ways. How strange it seems that man should know and cherish the spark of eternity inside himself and yet not recognize his own infinity! The one requires the other, of course.

It may be objected that men of science and good will have long been struggling to rid man of the feeling that he has an eternal, let alone infinite, spirit within him. Certain sensible men declare that they do not feel immortal at all. But feeling immortal is not the same thing as feeling the spark of eternity within one. And the frog who tried to puff himself up to the size of an ox has nothing in common with the man who turns reverently inward gazing on his own infinity.

If a man denies the spark of eternity within himself it may be only because he prefers to cherish that spark in private. Perhaps what he really objects to is the notion that his eternity can be arranged and provided beforehand like a Sunday picnic—the Sunday when Clarissa joined the choir and naughty Tom fell head-first into the bonfire.

But what if a logical man, asserting the patent mortality and limited extension of his own flesh, should repeat as simple fact that he has not, does not, and will not ever recognize a spark of eternity—let alone infinite space—within himself? That man is either mad or dead. It is as if a man honestly claimed to be a crocodile. He might prove logical enough, and reason from the width of his grin, the sharpness of his teeth, his general scaliness and swimming ability, yet he would also prove insane.

Logic—that ruinously expensive subway of human advance—tunnels straight in through the bright wilderness of space and time. Logic is no more open to illimitable winds than a subway is to the stars. Subways may be essential, but so are the wide-wandering paths of air.

These paths art provides: art keeps showing the truth

that along with the spark of eternity man also has infinite space within his spirit. This infinity no philosopher or priest, no one, can even try to map, arrange, appropriate. Only the artist comes and says, "Look inward, through what I have done, into your own starry heavens, yours alone."

Saint John by Leonardo, at the Louvre, seems menacing at first—a malignant Bacchus. His limbs form a spiral like the whirling sun surprised on its mysterious eastward passage home under the earth. Softly shining and coolly smiling, a night-eyed figure, he bars the way as he sits whirling and pointing in the dark forest. He might almost seem to be an angel of death, but no: he is an angel of inward life; he only bars the outward way.

Leonardo's *Madonna of the Rocks* nearby is like all the winds and rivers flown together, and she wears the crescent moon at her breast. The cave surrounding her is not a compositional device but a spiritual emblem. It represents the hollow of a man's skull, and also infinity.

One's inward knowing of eternity is almost always confirmed in life. The moment at noon under the pear tree as a child. Swimming alone on a calm night once in youth. Knowing, suddenly, in the moment before an all-important struggle, that one is fated to win. Knowing one's true love, sometimes. Holding one's own sick child at dawn and feeling him breathe easy again as the fever loosens its grip. Or walking with that same child, cured, down an April road with sky in the puddles. At such moments the spark of eternity blazes up inside and fills the darkness of the self with light.

To find infinity is rarer, and yet sometimes a good dream will lead a person inward up the dark interior streets, in through gates of rust and thorn, through a forest of terrors higher into the cool, and then along a rocky headland path to the world's brink within. Or, they say, to feel one's baby kicking in the womb. Or to gaze up at the stars and think how small one is—and think again, and smile. For a man is neither small nor large; he is dust, as nothing, yet infinity finds room there.

Of all the myriad, many-windowed rooms in the city of art, the Bruegel Room at Vienna may well command the broadest view. Taken into one's own being, it can open a new continent.

Bruegel's painted spaces, like Leonardo's, arc away inward from the picture surface to a far, far-distant vanishing, only to reappear out of the mist at the back of one's own mind and come folding forward, filling mile on mile with snowy light. It is rather as if Bruegel's space were a figure-eight, with oneself its astonished center.

The foreground of Bruegel's *January* is a snowy slope falling away from one's own high watching-place. Below, a weary huddle of hunters, empty-handed, slowly descends. The eyes of the men are bent upon the ground; the hounds curl their tails forlornly. The hunters are about to pass an inn with a picture sign outside—a stag bearing a cross between its antlers—which identifies it as Saint Eustace's. When the saint saw the vision between the stag's antlers, he gave up hunting. Will these hunters halt at the inn, or even raise their snow-dazed eyes to the sign? It is doubtful.

Below in the dusk lies a mill with its frozen water-wheel. People are skating, dark and spry, on the pond. In the milky distance stands a village church—centered and yet empty. Beyond that, a house is burning; tiny figures run to the rescue. Then comes the purple forest, and finally, far away, are lifting and climbing hand over hand the icy-fingered and snow-knuckled Alps. As a whole, the scene is frozen, forlorn, cruel, remote. And yet one feels the presence of a certain hope, impalpable as breath upon the clean air.

Three things are missing, and until one's own imagination participates to the extent of bringing these three things to the picture, it will forever remain a mystery. This was Bruegel's way—to make all men brothers in the creative process. The heroes of his pictures are always invisible. One has to re-create them within oneself. In the case of *January* it is oneself first of all that seems to be missing from the picture. Here is no resting-place, no comfort, and no warmth. The self swims bewildered, gazing down through freezing salt-green air.

Second, the stag is missing, since he was not caught. He stands in a glistening thicket on a slope overlooking the picture—more noble than anything therein. His antlers shine like polished candelabras, his ears with their delicate hairs prick up, and his black nostrils are faintly steaming. His golden eyes survey the silver scene, the backs of the defeated hunters, retreating, and the long, cold, curled tails of their wretched hounds. He must wonder why dogs follow men: tame animals mystify wild ones. Does the stag feel anything of triumph? No, but firmness, freedom, silence and rightness—all of these. Only man creaks and howls down the valley like breaking ice; only man is strange.

The Infant Jesus is missing because not yet known to more than a few, though He may be somewhere close by the Inn. It is January—near Twelfth-Night perhaps—and the world's love still frozen over. Weary, pitiful, murderous men, shall we no more go hunting?

If Cézanne did "Poussin over again from nature," Bruegel did Bosch over again from human nature. His *Children's Games* is Bosch's *Millennium* at a childhood level—the level of scraped knees, swift sobbings, exploratory joys and complete instinctive understanding of almost everything that matters.

Bruegel's pictures are themselves a kind of game, hopscotching inward to revelation. Or they are like elaborate dances of the soul, such as might be thought impossible in a "static" medium. But paintings from the hand of genius need be no more static than a symphony.

The right hand is the doer, and the left the dreamer. With doing and dreaming hands outstretched towards the *Children's Games,* what does one see? The right-hand way, increasingly aggressive, leads at last to a burning at the stake, far down the street. The left-hand way goes by hide-and-seek and blind-man's-buff, and pass-the-thimble—by widening curves and circles ever outward towards infinity. It has no stop.

Finally there is *The Egg Stealer.* A stream meanders from a distant farmhouse to coil about the foreground of this little Eden, and to intercept a stumbling oaf. Unaware that he is due for a ducking, the oaf points scornfully back across his shoulder at a youth who is climbing a tree to get at a nest. There is a sack of eggs already on the ground. The stream doubles back upon itself, under a caving bank. What is one to make of all this?

With Bruegel it is always a matter of "seek and ye shall find." Where lies this treasure—in an egg? The pictured space itself is egg-shaped, like the world sometimes. Prehistoric stone eggs have been found incised with encircling serpents—symbols of rebirth, perhaps—as the stream embraces this space. But perhaps the treasure is an empty nest, or perhaps it is tolerance enough to smile on foolishness and scorn alike—who can tell? But then, what is there so foolish, necessarily, about the egg-stealer climbing the tree? He seems foolish at first sight only because the oaf, whom one saw first, appears to find him so. And who would imitate an oaf's contempt?

Or is he such an oaf after all: this big sleepy fellow on the bank of the stream? Gaze long enough and he begins to change: like the bride in *The Wedding Feast,* he is mantled with glory before one's eyes. What had seemed a dull look fills with understanding; what had seemed a scornful smile fills with tenderness; what had seemed a clownish form fills with grace, like a god. One must hold in one's eyes this peasant Proteus until he reveals his true nature. Then afterwards ask and demand where lies the treasure, the secret of the Eden he guards.

He smiles, so tenderly now, and is silent. He points back across his shoulder; he steps out over the stream. One might take him for Bruegel himself: a man fulfilled, pointing back to his own youth as he steps off the Earth's edge into the stream of eternity, saying goodbye. There is a sackful of eggs on the ground: his life work it may be. The world has not been poor in creative works, not for millennia, yet one tries to add what one can: perhaps he is making a gentle joke about this. Or he may be saying that the stream curling under the overgrown bank will somehow bear him back to life again so that he will once more climb the tree in youth. Perhaps, perhaps; none of it satisfies. Bruegel was too big a man to make himself the center of a mystery. He had too much respect for mystery to pose before a mirror in masquerade.

Yet is there not something mirrorlike about this picture, a convex mirror, perhaps? And the oaf who became like a god: is there not something in his very transformation to think about? He smiles; he almost seems to be laughing. His foot hovers over the water. Shall I too plunge into the stream? Undoubtedly, but that can't be it. He points back across his shoulder. That also I can do, and I will imitate him; like a faithful mirror since he appears so wise. I stand on one foot, I point back across my shoulder. He does laugh now, and I turn to see where I am pointing.

Reality! The world!

And so the infinite flows back into the world, this sacred world.

Index